Dear Archbishop

Dear Archbishop

by

John Poulton

HODDER AND STOUGHTON
LONDON SYDNEY AUCKLAND TORONTO

Foreword

by

the Archbishop of Canterbury

VERY SOON AFTER I became Archbishop of Canterbury in December 1974 a steady stream of letters began to reach me, calling for a Day of Prayer for the nation. That letters with this request should be addressed to me came as no surprise, and I answered them in the way in which for a few years the Archbishops had thought right — namely to point to the greater value of Christian people praying regularly for our country rather than organise a national Day of Prayer.

It soon became clear, however, that these appeals for prayer indicated a deep longing for a better Britain on the part of a great many people, and that sooner or later some kind of lead ought to be given. These people needed a voice. My conviction was reinforced by visits paid to me by some people of influence in Britain who specifically asked that I should speak to the nation. It was a tall order, not least because I was urged to remember that time was short. The national situation was deteriorating. It was not next year that a call would have to be made, if it was made at all. July was suggested, and it was already April.

This being so, any idea of lining up all the leaders of the various Churches in Britain to hammer out an agreed message was ruled out. The best that could be hoped for was to inform the leaders of other Churches of what the Archbishop of York and I hoped to do, and to obtain their goodwill. In the event this was readily forthcoming.

Another difficulty was how to speak to as large a number of the British people as possible. Suggestions of a call to prayer from a great cathedral service, or even from a back-street church in one of our large industrial cities, were rejected on the grounds that the impression would thus be given that the Call was for Church people only. Attention therefore was turned to the broadcasting media and to the press, and here sincere appreciation must be recorded of their readiness to respond. We were advised that the best course was not to seek for special time at a peak hour when the Archbishop should speak to the nation on all channels, but rather to avail ourselves of space willingly offered in normal broadcasting programmes over a period of three or four days, so as to achieve something like saturation coverage. This meant that some forty million people would hear the message.

July proved too soon for the necessary preparations to be made, and so 15th October was finally suggested as the date for the Call to be launched. This followed the party political conferences and preceded the new session of Parliament. It was agreed that the Call should be made from my home at Lambeth Palace in London with full press coverage. Because this was the form the programme would take, fairness to the press required that the information should not be leaked beforehand.

So the Call to the Nation was made by means of what is popularly called the media. But because it was the Arch-bishops of Canterbury and York who were calling, Church congregations had to be included in some special way. This was the reason why the Pastoral Letter was read in all churches on the Sunday following. It was never meant to be more than a supporting letter, the main message having been given through the media. Because this point was not appreciated some misunderstanding arose.

What was the message? If you turn to Chapter One of this book you will find the text as it was delivered at the press conference on 15th October. You will also find the text of the Pastoral Letter read in the churches. Because part of the Call was a call to prayer on behalf of the nation, the text of the prayer card is also included. Some 80,000 of these prayer cards were eventually requested.

But why the letters? How did they come to be written? Quite simply, because in the broadcasts following the press conference I invited my listeners to write. I did this because I wanted to break through to ordinary people and make them feel that they matter. I wanted them to know that what they think counts. I also wanted to give a chance to what is often called 'the silent majority'.

What happened? Letters arrived at Lambeth Palace by the sackful, so that after about ten weeks the total was 27,000. This is quite a large number. But suppose that, for every person who wrote, a hundred meant to write but never 'got round to it' (and this is the normal estimate made in broadcasting circles). Then between two and three million British people reacted positively to the Call. The number would be increased to something like four million if the same method were adopted for the letters also received by the Archbishop of York, because from the very first he also took a full and active part in this whole enterprise.

Obviously we have in these letters a unique source of information about what people themselves are looking for in British life today — not what some leaders imagine they are looking for, or what they ought to look for, but what actually are their aspirations and their fears. Nor should the spontaneity of the letters be overlooked: they were not written as answers to a questionnaire. This is important.

In my judgment certain points stand out from these letters. Clearly I touched on a raw nerve when I suggested that the individual feels that he does not count as he should in our mass society. Evidently the frustration in our national life is acute at this point, almost bordering on despair. This is serious, because when national morale is as low as this, political and social planning, however reasonable, tends to become ineffective. The individual must feel that he counts. It is because there exists such widespread doubt about this that democracy is thought to have failed.

Secondly, this correspondence makes me anxious about

the position of the family in Britain today. The family is the basic unit in the nation; if this is weak the national life is weak. It is apparent, however, that what the majority of British people look for is a decent home and happy family life. What is more, they actually judge the quality of life available to them by this simple yardstick. What a change would be brought about if more of our social and political planners asked as a first question: 'How will this policy benefit home and family life in Britain?' I observe that John Poulton, the author of this book, suggests a Consultation to look into this matter along the lines of a fascinating operation now under way in British Columbia in Canada. At any rate, an urgent and determined new look seems necessary.

Thirdly, it is clear that a fresh attitude to work will have to be formulated. Instead of work being thought of as a burden to be avoided, it will have to be conceived as a benefit or a blessing to be shared out. Automation must mean fewer jobs. People know this. Here is a field in which radical thinking is called for which will affect our attitudes to education, the working week, wages, leisure and much else.

I would emphasise that the response received through the correspondence came from all sections of society. Church people wrote and non-Church people; quite a few began 'I do not know how to address an Archbishop' — just as if I minded! Letters came from young and old, management and men on the shop-floor, doctors, farm-workers, house-wives, school-teachers, pensioners, children — you name it, somewhere there will be a representative of that group among the letters. I was particularly glad to note how all branches of the Christian Church were represented, and to hear from Jews as well as from adherents of other religions. I gathered that a great deal of thinking was already going on up and down the country, seeking for a better way of life. This is what I wanted to encourage, and there is evidence that it is taking place on a very considerable scale.

To all who have been alerted by the Call and what has followed its launching, I would say this: 'Do not lose hope.

There is a great deal of potential among our people. With the grace of God, who knows what may not be achieved if we set our minds to purposeful and unselfish living?'

To Christians I would say this: 'Get fully involved in the discussion of the questions: "What kind of society do we want?" and "What kind of people are needed to create such a society?" Then, since you believe Jesus Christ to be the Way, the Truth and the Life, point people directly to him — with sympathy, understanding and intelligence. If we believe that he is the source of our salvation, that he alone can free us from the shackles of sin and of death and Hades, then let us say so, humbly and confidently. Humbly, for we know only too well that we are not the best advertisements for what Christians stand for and for the claims they make. Confidently, because we know of no other way that can be compared with him, no other truth that gives a like key to the meaning of life here and hereafter, no other life which can be called eternal life. Let us challenge our questioners — do they know a better way? To whom would they go? It is Christ, and Christ alone, who has 'the words of eternal life'.

Now that England is talking about issues of moment in a way that it has not done for a very long time; now that men are beginning to glimpse the truth that Jesus was right when he said that man cannot live on bread, on mere material things, alone, it is time for them to be challenged with the prophetic challenge: 'If the Lord be God, then serve him; if Baal, then serve him.' Make up your mind, one way or another.

Let us not be fearful that such a challenge is divisive. It needs must be. The Prince of Peace came to bring a sword — such is the paradox at the heart of our faith, and we must not shrink from it. It is a great moment when a man, in the desperation of his own sinfulness and hopelessness, cries out: 'Lord, to whom else can I go? You have the words of eternal life.' That desperation is the way to new birth.

Lambeth Palace,   DONALD CANTUAR:
London, SE1 7JU.

Acknowledgments

The Archbishop of Canterbury and the author are grateful not only to those whose letters are quoted in this book, but to the many thousands of other correspondents whose insights and concerns they reflect.

They would also like to thank publicly the happy band of volunteers who slogged away at Lambeth between October 15th and Christmas 1975 opening the mail, sending out prayer cards, and, later on, doing the research without which this book could not have been written.

Quotations on pages 118–119 and 158–159 are from 'Convictions' by Donald Coggan (Hodder & Stoughton), and the author and publishers thank S.P.C.K. for permission to make the quotation on pages 143–144 from the Archbishop's The Christian Faith.

A short study outline of this book has been published by the Archbishops' Council on Evangelism. Copies are available from Diocesan House, Quarry Street, Guildford, price 10p.

Contents

I

Why 27,000 Letters?

MOST BEGAN '*Dear Dr. Coggan*' because that was how it had been suggested people should write to him.

There were variations. '*My Dear Lord.*' '*Dear Sir.*' '*His Grace the Archbishop, dear Donald.*' Someone recalled 'a hilarious but irreverent moment from a Tony Hancock programme on the question "how to address oneself to an Archbishop", ' but the scriptwriters did not exhaust the possibilities seized by the public in October 1975!

'*Dear Archbishop*' came from all sorts of people. The widow who said, '*I never thought I should ever be writing to an Archbishop.*' Another who wrote, '*You seem different I hope your really are.*' Lord Mayors. Primary schoolchildren and sixth-formers. Families who did not go to church anymore. The R.C. lady who knew he was an Anglican but did not blame him for that. Trade Union branch secretaries. Rotarians. Some on glossy-headed business notepaper. The vast majority from home, from ordinary people wanting to say what was on their mind. Like the plater in a factory in Yorkshire who said, '*I do not usually write letters such as this, but in this case I felt I must.'* Or the housewife who was *'not in the habit of writing letters to the newspaper etc. but I feel I can identify with you; I feel you will understand.'*

The 'Call'

What had stimulated such a response? The Archbishop had called a press conference (with radio and TV there too), at his Lambeth home. **'I want to speak not only to members of the Churches', he had said, 'but to all those who are concerned for the welfare of our nation at a time when many thoughtful people feel that we are drifting towards chaos. Many are realising that a materialistic answer is no real answer at all. There are moral and spiritual issues at stake.**

The truth is that we in Britain are without anchors. We are drifting. A common enemy in two world wars drew us together in united action — and we defeated him. Another enemy is at the gates today, and we keep silence. We are afraid to speak out: it is time we spoke plainly.'

As the heart of the 'Call' he offered five statements.

1. EACH MAN AND WOMAN MATTERS

Each man and woman counts. Part of our trouble is that we think the individual is powerless. That is a lie. He is not powerless. Your

vote counts. Your voice counts. You count.
Each man and woman is needed if the drift
towards chaos is to stop. Your country needs
YOU.

2. THE FAMILY MATTERS

Give us strong, happy, disciplined families,
and we shall be well on the way to a strong
nation. The best way to cut at the roots of a
healthy society is to undermine the family. So
many young people who get into trouble with
the law come from broken homes. The family
matters, and it's worth working hard to build
it, protect it and provide for it.

3. GOOD WORK MATTERS

'A good day's work for a fair day's pay' isn't a
bad motto for worker and for management.
But pay isn't everything. 'Each for himself and
the devil take the hindmost' makes for chaos.
Guzzling doesn't satisfy. Grabbing and getting
is a poor creed. Envy is a cancer. Sacrifice is an
unpopular word; discipline even more so. But
without sacrifice, without discipline, and without a sense of responsibility at the heart of our
society, we're likely to perish. A bit of hardship
hurts none of us. Can you deny it? We're growing soft!

4. THE OTHER FELLOW MATTERS

I believe the only creed that makes sense is:
   God first —
   Others next —
   Self last.
   I see this worked out in the person and teaching of Jesus Christ. He has shown us the way — He gives us the power to follow it. And this is where prayer comes in.

5. ATTITUDES MATTER

Of course we need money. We must think about money, but if we think about nothing else except money — and we are getting dangerously near that sorry state today — the standards of our life will decline, yes, even in the material sphere! Stark materialism does not work. It does not deliver the goods. We must adopt a different attitude to money, and to materials and to machines. They are useful servants but they are degrading masters. It is the kind of people who handle them that matters and what their attitudes to life are. So stop making money the priority.

*   *   *

I am not offering a detailed plan or any kind of blueprint as a way out of her troubles for Britain. There are no easy answers to our problems. I do not pretend to know all the answers. But this is the point I want to make — unless there is a concerted effort to lift our whole national debate up into the moral sphere, not being afraid to ask individuals as well as the community what is right and what is wrong, we shall never find the answers. I am concerned for the spirit which is abroad in the country, because our national problems will not be solved unless we improve it.

I also want to encourage the enormous number of good people in Britain. They want a better country. They are saddened by the low level to which we have fallen. But they have no spokesman. It is the extremists who tend to receive the publicity, and often they win the round. What I am attempting is to strengthen this group of responsible people.

And here is a third aim. I want to see opening up all over Britain groups of men and women, of all denominations and of none, who will sit down and face these two questions: —
'What sort of society do we want?' and
'What sort of people do we need to be in order to achieve it?'

At first sight these questions seem extremely simple. But set them side by side and they imply something which to our great loss we have largely forgotten in our nation today — which is, that the sort of people we are makes the society we get. Put another way, it means that we cannot leave out the moral factor and

succeed *in the long run.* **It is in the light of this that I want to initiate this debate today. It is in the light of this overriding consideration that I want the groups to do their thinking, working at specific problems in their own localities.**

The same day, and in the week following, the Archbishop appeared on radio and TV seven times. The press gave extraordinary coverage to what he was saying. Nearly every editorial comment was appreciative and constructive. The debate which he had intended to develop had begun.

The Prayer

In the weeks that followed 27,000 letters poured in to Lambeth. A team of volunteers opened them, sent out the promised 'prayer-card', and put on one side those letters which called for personal answers. By Christmas 75,000 cards had been posted, for many who wrote in had asked for several copies, or for a stock of them for their church or association.

The prayer, which started up another wave of correspondence in its own right, read: —

> *God bless our nation,*
> *Guide our rulers.*
> *Give us your power,*
> > *that we may live cheerfully,*
> > *care for each other,*
> > *and be just in all we do.*

Based on an earlier one for Africa, this simple prayer had been written for use by as many groups as possible in contemporary Britain. Some church people objected, and wanted it much more pointedly 'Christian'. Others wondered why it was so Britain-centred when the rest of the world's needs were so tremendous.

Yet another series of letters asked why the Archbishop should imagine God had any further interest in so wicked a nation as we had now become. The only possible prayer would have been 'God avert your wrath', with apparently minimal faith that he would.

As it stood, the prayer was variously described as *'canting hypocritical humbug'*, *'beautifully simple'*, *'simple, yet all embracing'*. A doctor said, *'I am going to pin it on our surgery notice board.'* A retired business man referring to its brevity and directness, added, *'Your card, the prayer facing outwards, is on the mantelpiece of our bedroom. I am conscious of its presence and read it several times a day.'*

The Correspondents

It was plain from the word go that the Archbishop had made a very personal impact on many who saw or heard him, and on those who read about the 'Call' in the newspapers, or heard from friends later. (Sometimes a lot later, like the lady who *'was ill recently, and my neighbour brought me in the* Woman *in which you spoke about your "Call"* '.)

From a remote part of Scotland a lady wrote, '*It was just as if you were sitting by our fireside talking things over with us.*' A gentleman in Essex began '*Thanks for the pleasure of your company in my home last Sunday.*' A number of other letters started '*When you were speaking to us here the other day . . .*'

In part this was due to the Archbishop's style and the way his personality came across on the box. But more than that, as the whole correspondence showed, it was what he chose to say.

'*I listened to your speech on the television the other evening, and I feel that I speak for the majority of people when I say how pleased I was to know at last someone had the courage and strength to put into words what we are thinking.*'

The *Western Mail* commented, '*There must be thousands for whom Dr. Coggan has acted as a succinct and forceful spokesman.*'

The editorial went on, '*It is important to note that although he emphasised the rôle of prayer, he was not, as one M.P. remarked, "passing the buck to God in prayer". He was also calling upon us to slog it out. It was a call to people to act out in their lives spiritual convictions which may have lain dormant, a call for communal self-help and individual self-sacrifice.*'

The Pastoral Letter

On the Sunday after all this, a joint Pastoral Letter by the Archbishops of Canterbury and York was read in the parish churches. It underlined in more specifically Christian language what the 'Call' had been saying via the public media to the whole nation.

'During the last few days you will probably have shared through the media something of what we have been trying to say at this critical time. We have posed such questions as these — "What sort of society are we looking for?" and "What kind of people are needed for the creation of this society?"

We Christians believe that God reigns and that he cares about the nations.

We believe that he has demonstrated his concern in the life, teaching, death and resurrection of Jesus Christ.

We believe that his Spirit is operative today doing his re-creative work in individuals and groups. If, however, a responsible society is to come into being, everyone must realise that he counts and that his contribution matters.'

The last sentence rang the loudest bell in people's minds. Thousands refer to it (or to the same theme as it came in the 'Call' itself) as the moment of lift-off in their response to the Archbishop.

The Pastoral Letter went on:

'The time has therefore come when we feel it is our duty to call all Christian people:

(i) to pray steadily, persistently and intelligently for our nation.

(ii) to think seriously about our society in the light of what we believe, asking such questions as "What sort of society do we want?" and "What sort of people do we need to be in order to achieve it?".

(iii) to co-operate with Christians of every allegiance, and with any others who are willing to be associated with us, so as to influence society in a positive and helpful way.

(iv) to live out the faith we profess, that God reigns and that God cares.'

A great deal has happened in response to these specific challenges. The fact remains, however, that the man and woman in the street as well as in the pew, first heard and then wrote on the basis of the statement 'everyone must realise that he counts and that his contribution matters'. It was maybe this more than anything that lay behind what a psychiatric worker reported:

'*I saw a Baptist Church poster which simply said THANK YOU ARCHBISHOP. I endorse that.*'

2

Each Man and Woman Matters

Each man and woman matters

This statement touched an exposed nerve. The Archbishop almost need have said nothing else. As one mother wrote, for all her family, '*Thank you for voicing the thoughts and desires of millions of good ordinary people inside and outside the Church, and for giving us hope that there is something we as individuals can do. It is so easy to feel terribly inadequate in the face of the present situation, to feel that our little bit is so insignificant it isn't worth doing.*' Or this, from Berwickshire, '*It encouraged us more than I can possibly put into words to feel that you were appealing to us, in spite of our remoteness, to stand up and be counted.*'

A family in East Anglia saw the stress on the individual's responsibility as the key to our problems — '*We are convinced of the truth of your words.*' A professional man in London said it was '*this that caught my imagination*'. Pleading for a movement throughout the land, which might match the Wesleyan Revival, a correspondent said he saw every humble contribution to be important.

A non-Church Guide company leader wrote on behalf of '*a few of the individuals who believe everyone counts*', and said their Patrol Leaders' Council had decided to use the Archbishop's prayer as their Guide prayer.

A Service wife, recounting her feelings when in 1974 she returned to Britain after a number of years abroad ('*appalling apathy*'), went on, '*I felt just a glimmer of light when I first read your article. At last someone is going to point a finger and say "You can help". No one has yet stated the truth that the people of England are to blame for our situation today, always making excuses for what they have done wrong.*'

A factory-hand would '*not agree with what seems to be a majority opinion, that the individual does not count*'. And a senior civil servant wrote, '*It is within the power of the individual to influence the course of his own life: he is both allowed to use, and uses, his head. We may all be fanned by the same breeze, but the right to put on or take off sail is ours.*'

Quite a number echoed the Archbishop's reference to World War II in his 'Call', and said anything can happen once there is a cause to follow, '*The human family needs a purpose for leading the good life, and to feel assured that individually they are needed ... We are ordinary people, human and frail, but there is nothing we cannot do if we work with the power God gives to us.*'

From Cambridge came a more basic observation. '*The problem of the relevance of each ordinary man to society, and to affect events, lies at the root of the hopelessness many feel. But he or she is unique (as even an identical twin or a thumbprint is unique). How then can anyone claim to be*

*other than influential? We are able to influence life and
unable not to.'*

'You can't mean it'

At no point were those who wrote to the Archbishop
all of one mind. A married nurse whose work takes
her into the community in a Midland town, commented, *'Unlike yourself I am powerless to make even a
small ripple in the "river of life", which seems to flow faster,
caring little which way it twists and turns.'*

A member of the House of Lords echoed her. *'Most
people feel themselves to be wage-slaves (I know, I am one of
them) and that the business of surviving and enjoying their
leisure is all they are prepared to do. Others say, "What can I
do? I work all day and I am too tired in the evening for
voluntary work, and even if I did do something it would be so
inadequate that it is hardly worthwhile." '*

Many correspondents told how they had lost
heart at the hands of the legal profession. Some told
stories going back over frustrating years of crippling
expense. Many shared how their treatment in
court and in the solicitors' offices had beaten them
into the ground at a time when a cynically professional comment was the last thing on earth they
needed.

Nor was this only in connection with divorce pro-
ceedings, though that came up again and again.
Ordinary people usually turn to the law only in
emergency, seeking what seems to them a common-
sense redress for a grievance, or a friendly word of

advice. The correspondence showed how often they go away empty-handed.

For others the moment of despair had been the illness of a relative or the death of someone very close. Few said that in these circumstances they had felt bereft by God. They were more concerned about the way it all seemed to add up to a pointlessness already so obvious in life as they had to live it today.

There were those who had tried, and come to grief. *'More than once,'* wrote an old lady in London, *'I have helped someone in distress. Just recently I gave a young man refuge, food and money. To my regret he repaid me by robbing me of money and jewellery. I had to call the police to get him to leave . . . What appals me is friends and the police behave as if I have been at fault, and their question is impertinent, "Why do I trust people?" To me the real trouble today is no one trusts. How can you find peace in a world of suspicion? . . . But probably I shall do the same again. I have never forgotten Christ's words.'*

A voluntary social worker wrote, after being *'manoeuvred out of office'*; *'None know the price of standing up and being counted faster than those who serve the nation within the walls of bureaucracy. I do not count my fate as outstanding in being removed from my work-day post for opening my mouth and going to my M.P. about certain hospital procedural goings-on.'*

For many who wrote, the frustrations were personal and total. The Archbishop had to be in another world, or he could not believe the individual mattered still.

'This morning I was in tears of frustration as I listened to the review of the papers just before your interview with

Clive Jacobs on "Sunday". 220,000 tons of apples are to be destroyed in France because they are "surplus". How can God bless our nation or the E.E.C. when we wantonly destroy his bountiful provision? You tell me I matter, but I felt I could do nothing to stop the destruction. Holding up the traffic in Parliament Square or throwing rotten apples at Mr. Peart would achieve publicity, but I am pessimistic enough at the moment to believe that neither course would save the apples!'

Or from Newcastle. '*Our wishes on every possible important issue (e.g. immigration, the death penalty) are ignored. Who today listens to the voice of the British people? The law was meant to protect the common man, not to oppress him. You can't treat people in this way in their own land.*' (In the face of which another correspondent spelled out his answer — '*referendums, referendums and more referendums*').

And then there is Ulster. Letters from or about Northern Ireland were almost entirely in the same vein. We can do nothing: no one can do anything: therefore someone (and the Archbishop could be the 'someone') should do something soon.

A Belfast mother spoke for them all. '*Many of us in this unfortunate province are most anxious to live together in peace and harmony but find it so difficult to make our voices heard.*'

An under-employed Oxbridge graduate, having told his story, summed up the feelings of all those who could not accept the Archbishop's faith in the power of the individual '*What can I do about all this? It is like trying to swim in suet pudding.*'

'We'd like it to be true'

The other side to the coin was often the expression of wistful hope. '*Please tell me what to do because I am completely bewildered. Anything at all. Thank you for trying to help,*' wrote a wife in the North.

A family in Cheshire '*pray that your belief in the individual will be vindicated and that we will not let you down.*'

A housewife wrote, '*It is hard for me to watch and hope while people tear down everything I believe in (family life, democracy). I listen to it all happening, but what can I do? You have given me hope, but there must be hundreds of thousands of people you get through to. I really believe the meek shall inherit the earth, but do the meek really believe it?*'

An R.C. senior citizen in London called herself '*one of those ordinary everyday people you were just talking about on TV who dearly wish we could help to put our beloved country on a more even (and Christian) keel.*'

For many the wistfulness included a look back. '*I would dearly love to see once again the spirit we had in the two wars when we were fighting for our lives.*'

Someone else said she believed '*people are unhappy and unsettled when they have no great definite cause to make sacrifices for. Without such an objective people feel lost and useless and resort to various forms of irresponsible behaviour. Hence the terrorists, who believe they have a cause, and are prepared to fight and die for it.*'

But from Merseyside came perhaps the most moving expression. Writing from his wheel-chair (where '*the horizon is not vastly inferior from that of those who walk*'), the writer hoped that '*you just may be able to inspire those like myself of the more or less silent majority who have been unable to take up a specific religious affiliation yet are at heart religious. Those of us who find we cannot whole-heartedly and therefore honestly accept Christian theology but who nevertheless support those ethics which echo in the Scriptures of the great religions, sometimes feel in lonely isolation from others of our time. We have been so overwhelmed by politicians ill-advising to produce more until the bubble has burst, that we have developed a convenient psychological deafness. Yet . . . If only, if only . . .*'

'*This is how it works*'

'*I know we have it within ourselves to put things right,*' wrote a Yorkshire housewife. And a ninety-two-year-old in the West Country: '*I know God has much that I can do to back you up.*'

These represent the substantial number of those who felt we had done enough blaming of others and indulging in self-pity. The Archbishop received a number of copies of the sturdy and down-to-earth *Housewives' Declaration*, which said:

We will tackle today's difficulties as a challenge and not depress others with our grumbling.
We will care about the standard of living and true happiness of families across the world. Have we the right to get richer every year when so many are hungry?
We accept that food will cost more everywhere. We are ready to spend less on luxuries. We will

shop for need and not from greed or for hoarding and will re-think how much is enough for us.

We will refuse to let the hurts and bitterness or entrenched attitudes of the past shape our future. We will accept honestly our own share of the blame for our present troubles. (Copies from Mrs K. Evans, Whitbourne, Worcester)

Hundreds also referred to ACTION 75 ('a serious attempt by ordinary people to inspire a nation-wide response to the conception of "A Year for Britain rather than a Year for Self" '). As one writer put it, *'our aim is to make vocal the voice of the silent majority and to put democracy on the offensive. We want to see Britain governed by men governed by God.'* They set out, with considerable trade union support, to get a million signatures to their statement.

Some were able to illustrate their faith in what the individual can do. *'I am particularly grateful for your insistence on the importance of individuals "leavening" a situation. I have recently known of this happening — in Cyprus, where one man's calmness prevented a crowd panicking and leaving their homes, and in Northern Ireland, where a Protestant woman refused to boycott Catholic tradespeople and the whole street followed her example.'*

An artist, designer and illustrator wrote from Scotland: *'The West is intellectually strong, but spiritually and mystically weak. I do believe that each one of us may help in this so important matter, every single one: by showing goodwill to one's fellow men and women, and attempting to live a harmless life (positive harmlessness — the Buddhists have a word for it), and thus ending separatism, or this cult of difference between people, nations and beliefs.'*

The managing director of a London restaurant brought it down to brass-tacks: *'Our personnel training manager came to see me and said, "Could we make a job for another trainee cook?" We stopped and tried to find God's direction knowing that every additional expense decreases profitability, but also that our policy has always been to put people before profits, giving a service that answers the needs of our community and country. Here was a national need. The careers officer fell on our necks. "Oh," she said, "could you possibly take two trainees? When young people come in here I cannot look them in the face as I have nothing to offer them, thank you for ringing us." She continued, "I have a girl who has been waiting for a year to be a cook, taking odd jobs to fill in the time." Jennifer has now started with us, and has the makings of a first-class cook. Her mother is a widow with eight children.*

'I was speaking with one of our restaurant customers about this situation in industry, and the unwillingness to take trainees because the apprentice so often moves to another firm immediately he is trained. His conviction was "that every good employer should feel he has a duty to make a contribution to the industry as a whole." "That concern for the individual," he said, "is part of a general attitude which includes a desire to serve and to provide good value. This is reflected in the quality of the product of one's efforts, which in turn produces an economic reward." '

What is being said here, again and again, is that people sense that they must see the achievement any man or woman can make alone in terms of its quality

and potential for good. 'Success' can only be a sign
of what might be; the beginnings of growth from a
small seed. Life around seems too complex for bigger
ideas to feel right — or to 'feel' at all.

Look at it through one man's eyes in London. '*I
travel a great deal on public transport where it is noticeable,
especially during the rush hour, that nearly everyone goes
about as though* blind: *a woman carrying a baby, a shopping bag and a folding pram will go unheeded and have to
fend for herself.*' He adds, '*We live in a "do-it-yourself"
world,*' but only because he has seen that '*thirty
million people (or any number you like!) doing small acts of
kindness and thoughtfulness to each other daily will create a
vastly different climate to the present one where self-interest
and indifference to others is more of a habit than a vice.*'

'*More of a habit*'

How to account for the habit? There are clues in
what people say. Here are three. They are some of
the stress-points on individuality in our society. Because of them many find the Archbishop's statement
'Every man and woman matters' hard to take. They
are all 'me and them' areas of life. Ordinary me and
big impersonal, uncontrollable, faceless them.

I. THE MAMMOTH GROUPINGS

These include the nationalised industries as they
impinge on ordinary individuals with ever-mounting
bills for goods and services the family cannot do
without and cannot get from anywhere else. They

matter also because of their vast deficits which are debts being incurred on our behalf, because in the end these industries and the government of the day cannot create resources of their own. Someone has to pay, and there is a shrewd suspicion it includes 'ordinary me.'

Similarly, the departments of government which administer health, pensions and the other social benefits. Many correspondents felt that through these institutions every man and woman was seeking justice and well-being for every other man and woman in an organised social system. They knew this was right. Yet at the interface between public and administrator, they knew also what could happen.

Fear of officialdom causes many ordinary people to be provocative and awkward to 'them'. And since people are people (specially 'them' people), the reaction calls forth all too often what had been expected. So a lady could write: *'We have to get our government, local government — and hospitals — to take up a new approach towards people. Good manners, care and attention, no matter who it is who approaches them, give people back some respect.'*

This has to work both ways. Correspondents who voiced the *'no one knows me'* feeling when talking of these aspects of life in our country today, seemed unaware of the 'no one loves me' other side of the office or reception desk encounter. Nor, it must be said, did all the critics of the politicians (the ultimate 'them' group) preserve this understanding and acceptance of them as people doing a job as best they can.

From Welwyn came the shrewd comment, *'I have
no illusions as to the vast difficulties in waking ordinary folk
to the problems which we have created for ourselves as a direct
result of choosing to live in a technological society with all its
material gains and loss of individual identity.'*

2. THE MEDIUM-SIZED GROUPINGS

A Midlands mother wrote: *'I can't help feeling that
the tragedy of life today is that people feel they no longer
matter, everyone is lost in the "bigness" of everything. Shops
go from super to hyper, local authorities group together to
take in larger and larger areas, and schools are quite dis-
gustingly huge. If only we could be made to realise that
our individual behaviour matters, however small we might
feel.'*

Shops (with the corner shop going out of business);
local government (new names, larger areas than feel
like 'us'); schools (requiring head staff to be admini-
strators on a scale that can destroy confidence in that
personal-ness we had always assumed was the essential mark of a teacher). Again and again his correspondents drew the Archbishop's attention to their
frustrations in these very important parts of their
lives.

*'We heard Ed Burman describing on "Woman's Hour" a
group called "Inter-Action", and their "City Farm" in
Camden Town. Several of the boys who help run the farm
were interviewed; it sounded a splendid and most successful
place.*

*'And then Mr. Burman told us that the farm was under
threat because the land it stands on will be wanted for*

"development"! It is this sort of unimaginative bureaucratic action on the part of "Councils" which makes people feel so helpless.'

This does, on the other hand, illustrate one of the ways increasingly used now to try to make things change.

Certain programmes on radio and TV are always eager to air grievances or publicise apparent non-senses by 'them', on behalf of ordinary people. The fact that the letter about Camden Town came from Wales perhaps confirms the influence of such 'ex-posures'. The development of local radio has added to such possibilities. The use of already existing media of public communication, the press, radio, TV, posters, community or parish magazines, is not yet being fully exploited.

Many letters, like the one just quoted, referred to broadcasts in order to illustrate their points. *'On TV a few weeks ago, a young lad of about fifteen was being questioned about breaking a window. His reply was that he was a mere number at school where there were two thousand pupils. When he came out he felt the urge to do something to convince himself he was a person.'*

At other levels the same feelings are expressed by demonstrations and banners, or by violence during public enquiries when these are felt by protesters to be a charade.

'People don't matter. Motor cars; lorries; roads are much more important. Instead of making a by-pass for a lovely old medieval city, the traffic has to go through some very narrow streets. There is an almost continuous procession of long, heavy lorries, many of them European, passing

through. This depersonalisation of people is a sign of the times.'

Against a background of feelings like these, a men's group on Humberside *'felt that the whole of society needs to be "re-personalised". A society has to be created in which units are not too large. The man on the factory-floor does not know his employer; a child in a large Comprehensive School does not know and is not known by his teachers and head teacher; local newspapers are taken over by giants creating a situation in which editors have little knowledge of the people for whom they write.'*

Fear of size came through again and again in the letters, but always in defence of what is personal. Thus there were those parents who, voicing their doubts about large schools, paid warm tribute at the same time to the individual care and concern of some teachers and heads. There were those who were sad at the passing of the corner shop, but who also re-corded the warmth and friendliness of their local supermarket staff.

3. THE STRUGGLE TO STAY A PERSON

'Loneliness is the biggest scourge of our times', wrote a Londoner between jobs. *'We do not play a part in anything, or form a part of anything'*.

A social worker said she believed *'a good proportion of the population have never felt themselves to be loved and therefore do not see themselves as lovable and have a poor sense of themselves as people. The only way they exist in their own eyes is either to cause a nuisance and, through others taking notice of them, reinforce their own slender identity, or to collect possessions so that they have an existence in relation to them.'*

At many points the scale of things, referred to in the previous section, emphasises this lostness. As has been said often enough before, when you are a case to your G.P., a hand to your boss, a computerised account untouched by the hand of your friendly bank manager, another category of case if you fall foul of the law, or stand in need of help from the social services, you have to work to preserve any sense of believing you are still a person.

So in letter after letter people pleaded *'go on helping people feel they count', 'develop this aspect of the value of the individual', 'emphasise personal relationships on which society depends'.*

Combining this with the point about the scale of things, a correspondent observed: *'Before one can be a good neighbour, one has to be a neighbour. Our capacity for neighbourliness is limited, and therefore our social life, commercial life and industrial life should try to break down the macrocosm into many microcosms, in each of which we stand in a personal relationship to other members, and they stand in a personal relationship to us. This is the kind of life the fortunate ones among us have enjoyed in small schools, family businesses, village life, cricket teams, regimental life and so on.*

'It has been said "Small is beautiful". To break up the large into the small will be difficult, but good schools and good regiments manage to combine unity of direction with small groups that are accorded a large measure of autonomy. Not all small groups are ipso facto instinctive with love, but even bickering and outbursts of temper are better and warmer

*than the impersonality and boredom of the monolithic struc-
ture.'*

A final aspect of how *'people are struggling, as never
before, for personal identity'*, involves the complex pressures on us of the advertising, media and marketing
worlds. In the next chapter we shall look at these in
detail, but they should not be omitted at this point.

A writer from Oldham saw them as a sort of mass-
attack on the person: *'The power of advertising never
ceases to amaze me. Every day articles are presented in the
most colourful and attractive manner, while we are told to
envy our neighbours' goods, and to obtain the various items
in order to live the "good" life. To what extent can that be
said to respect the integrity and dignity of the individual?'*

Many writers were quite plainly struggling with
this, and aware that an answer on a purely personal
level only might be impossible. We are dealing here
with the whole dynamic of the capitalist economy.
Yet, wrote an R.C. mother from London, although
*'nobody likes the perversities and injustices of the capitalist
society, any more than Christ can have liked the excesses of
Roman society . . . he called the individual to follow him and
did not merely rant at the Roman Emperors.'*

A good many went on at the Archbishop, usually
about others. The bosses, the bishops, the Reds, the
extremists, the unions, the unacceptable faces of
capitalism and of any other system currently on offer.
Significantly, nearly every argument was based on
the worth of every man and every woman, and the
failure so far to find a political system in which this
could be fully expressed. Yet the very strength with
which even diametrically opposite political views

were being expressed, illustrated the deep human longing that the Archbishop's statement should be true and be seen in our society to be true. Here was a first guide-line for the sort of society people wanted.

Questions

1. How many local Council employees do I *know*? What helps or hinders them in doing a good job?

2. Are there real limits on being personal in my work relationships? Why?

3. In what parts of my life (citizen, member of groups or associations, etc.) do I sometimes *vote*? What value do I put on this? In what sense do I feel myself responsible for decisions made by those I elected?

4. '*I have no illusions as to the . . . problems* we have created for ourselves *as a direct result of choosing to live in a technological society with all its material gains and loss of individual identity.*' What do you say in answer to the phrase 'we have created for ourselves'? Think of one such problem which involves a loss of individual identity (e.g. administering a *national* social service of any kind), and decide on one or two ways in which locally you could do something about it.

5. Are you going to do something about it?

6. What does all this suggest about the nature of human beings? What is so important about the individual anyway?

3

The Family Matters

'*It was hard enough to bring up my own children against outside pressures, but I am even more concerned for the future of my grandchild.*' This from Cheshire.

From Newcastle a mother wrote, '*I find it difficult to express my feelings in words, but the future is frightening . . . we seem to be losing our way.*' The word 'frightening' comes again and again as people look at life and talk about their children's future.

Another family in the North said, '*They are so real these fears for our children. The way we are heading, what will our country have to offer them not just in education, jobs, money, but in things like learning to live and love and communicate with people? Will they ever get the chance to choose for themselves?*'

'*One is seized with despair, and a feeling of helplessness and defeat, all wrong, I know, for Christians.*' That from Wales.

What are people afraid of?

It is worth analysing this very general sense of fear
which so many expressed. Someone from Yorkshire
opened it up like this:

*'Since 1960 I have seen such a change in the world that
I feel I cannot accept it. The young people of this day and
age have such a different way of life to mine that it seems
that everything I have been brought up to believe in has been
wrong. The people in England have had their spirit broken
by the pressures and the conning they have suffered. We seem
to be living at such a pace it makes one feel we are rushing
towards the inevitable.'*

One might sympathetically write 'Future Shock'
against such a *cri de coeur*, but to categorise or name a
state of mind does nothing to meet the condition.

Others were more specific in describing their fears.
*'Let us fight against the dark forces of anarchy and com-
munism, of chaos and greed, and of the devil . . .' 'for we
wrestle not against flesh and blood, but against principalities
and powers,'* wrote a student from a college in the
North-West.

The fear of communism expressed in that letter,
was spelled out in many others. The writers saw the
'menace of this godless threat' already well-entrenched in
British society, and some blamed it not only for industrial disruption but also for a deliberately planned
programme of moral corruption, whereby our present democratic ways could be finally destroyed. The
attack, in other words, on stable family life, was
integral to the ultimate political revolution, and

many of the Archbishop's correspondents were fearful of the signs of its success which they recognised all around. '*Little by little we have seen the erosion of the whole Christian basis of our school.*'

'*The permissive society . . . the corrupting of the minds of our children by teachers, family planning and TV — violence, sex-ridden films under the guise of education, and the teaching of Christianity, not as such, but merely as one of many religions, by those who do not believe in it.*'

But all the letters were not anti-communist by any means. Large numbers used very similar 'crusading' terms against the evils of capitalism. So far as the family is concerned, it is equally devastating, claimed many writers, that young mothers have to go out to work, leaving their children to fend for themselves; that the obscenities of homelessness are matched by the appalling conditions in which so many are housed; and that the dehumanising effects of unemployment on the home are so little realised or cared about.

These political angles were not people's only concern. What we are doing to our environment was another. From the Lake District a couple very much aware of their own blessings, commented, '*So many people live in towns and squalid quarters, becoming depressed for sheer lack of interest. They never see the seasons.*'

And from a council estate in Dorset, a mother with much to contend with wrote, '*Please try and stop the motorway coming. When will the destroying stop? Our flowers are getting oh, so rare, and who can speak for flowers, birds, and animals? Surely all things have a right to grow and live? But the greed of the rich who just want a holiday*

*or weekend cottage breaks down the bank that held so many
of our rarer flowers. They plant roses instead. Then the deer
must go, as they fancy the roses. And the moles. And the
badgers . . . I do pray, "Lord let our children's children see
all the beauty you gave for me to see".'*

Inflation was another concern. Not so much for the
suffering it causes, as for its coarsening effects on life;
the way, especially in the heart of the family, it causes
us to concentrate on material things rather than on
quality of living.

A Surrey man writes *'When you spoke of selfishness, I
think the reaction of many must have been "I'm not demand-
ing higher wages (or profits or dividends) for my own sake,
but in order that my wife may have a better home, so that I
can send my children to university or start them on their
careers." Thus the family can be regarded as a "self", and
can be selfish in its view of life.*

*'We spend many millions of pounds out of taxation and
local rates to enable people to opt out of responsibility for
their neighbours. This is an important part of the cause of
inflation. We need to cultivate a wider concept of the family
as a centre of love and concern for others.'*

What sort of home life do we want?

In saying **'Give us strong, happy, disciplined
families, and we shall be well on the way to a
strong nation',** the Archbishop had clearly touched
a second exposed nerve in the nation. There were
many who welcomed this 'Call', and wanted him to
say more.

A couple in the West Country listed the positive things that would be gained by a renewed commitment to stable home life. '*The individual can count in the family. It is a small enough community. It brings all age groups together without having to create an artificial situation to do so. The family is the first solution to the problem of loneliness at any age. It gives day-to-day reality to ideals that otherwise wither for lack of practical outlets.*'

Three main descriptions of a good family emerged from the hundreds of letters which concentrated on this point in the 'Call'. Happy home life teaches and embodies discipline, love and caring. It is the natural 'school' where all these are learned in the doing of them.

DISCIPLINE

Discipline got a very good press, all things considered. '*A basic necessity of a happy country.*' '*One is being kinder to one's children to discipline them than to allow free expression. Only so will they learn full self-discipline, without which there can be no law and order in the home, the school, in a career or in the country and world at large.*'

'*We were taught as children to respect our parents and those in authority over us, which prevented us from wanting to pull down everything we did not like.*'

'*I am certain that children need a framework of order and discipline both at home and at school. This must be carried on right through adolescence and only slackened gradually as the child learns to discipline himself. With love and concern and understanding (and self-sacrifice on the part of the parents) this need not be a painful process, as I have proved with my family of six.'*

'I was brought up by my parents to do my duty, to be honest, and to consider my fellow-men and their feelings. I was taught that "this was right, this was wrong", and I developed a conscience accordingly. This attitude is now old-fashioned. It is now accepted that you should do just what you want to do, because if you don't have your own way, you suffer from nerves, or something. I feel a lot of unhappiness is caused by children being given their own way from the early days.'

How is discipline to be learned in these days? There were many with a simple family story to tell (mostly peppered with frank admissions of the times it hadn't worked, but on balance adding up to a way of life that had proved reasonably successful).

Keeping lines of communication open is one clue. A Methodist family in the Midlands referred to the strict discipline they had applied to their four children, and how strong a family tie had developed. *'My wife and I feel this ourselves, but many a time also others remark on how close we seem to be, and how the children seem to talk about their parents as their friends. We have tried to maintain a high moral standard without being old-fashioned. I believe our children have appreciated this as we can talk about sex, religion or whatever it may be without anyone being embarrassed by it.'*

Another family, in Hertfordshire said, *'With our children time spent in talking out various aspects of everyday life . . . is time well-spent.'*

The encouragement of pursuits that build in their

own training in self-control, self-discipline, is another clue to which some parents referred.

An East Anglian mother wrote, '*I think many young parents are trying to bring discipline into their children's lives, and the growth in membership of such organisations as the Cubs shows this. Other organised activities (in this area) are swamped with recruits. Gymnastics classes for the over-threes have had to be doubled, for the schools have given up formal gymnastics but the parents feel that the children need the exercise. A growing number of boys here go to dancing classes . . . the teacher is inspiring, the children have to do what they are told, are not influenced by their peers in the class, and are delighted to learn a technique and see improvement in themselves.*'

'Outward Bound' and various other organisations which work on that same motivation (encouraging young people to learn a technique and to take pride in self-improvement) had written, pledging support to the Archbishop's 'Call', it is worth noting here.

And if this all sounds too cosily middle-class, let it be recorded also that the mother in East Anglia had moved there from the edge of a new Glasgow housing area, and commented '*The people I admire were the ones in the middle of the 40,000 estate who still struggled to bring up their children decently, surrounded by what seemed positive encouragement to bad behaviour.*'

What's the alternative?

There was no lack of material on what happens when discipline breaks down. From every part of the country came letters each with a personal story.

A lady in South London told how '*the other week I was waiting for a local bus. A very modern school-girl was waiting too, to go to a nearby Comprehensive School, she told me. She was thirteen. I asked her if she liked the headmaster. She hesitated for a moment, then said, "He's too soft, you can get away with anything."* '

A working wife in another part of London reported how '*Three weeks ago my grandson who is thirteen was held, punched and kicked in the face by four boys who thought it was a joke. Going to the police we were told there was nothing they could do because it was his word against the others . . .*'

And from the Midlands, '*We are worried about many things — indiscipline in schools, complete lack of courtesy, the alarming rise in crime, and above all we are worried about violence. Violence and treating human life as of no consequence seems to be everywhere. Many of us would never have believed it could happen in English schools and in the streets of our towns.*'

From Merseyside, '*We are appalled at the landslide of morals in every walk of life: at the dishonesty, violence, permissiveness, lack of discipline and the continuing decline in law and order, futile sentences given to criminals, and so on.*'

From every part of the country from all denominations and from people specifically disavowing any church connection, came letters pin-pointing abortion as the great sin of our times. '*Murder*', '*blasphemy*', '*permissiveness run amok*'. At this spot the sensitivity of very large numbers of the Archbishop's correspondents was being trampled upon by what had come to be accepted in society.

Or had it really been accepted by most people? This was a question raised in letter after letter. '*What right have the government to ignore the deeply held convictions of vast numbers of us like this?* asked a mother in Scotland. '*How far can our M.P.s stray into areas touching ultimate religious scruples, and not take note of what a majority of the nation must surely still feel?*'

This raises again the problem of traditional Christian reactions in a society no longer overtly 'Christian'. During the time of the 'Call' many of the bishops took the occasion to speak on this issue. The Bishop of Dorking wrote, for instance: '*I sense that many feel the need for greater discipline in their personal lives. Those who begin a letter with that kind of observation often end up urging us to "bring back the birch". I have no such intention.*

'*The discipline which had been generated by World War II burst like a bubble in the mid-1950s. A new climate which we have come to call "agnostic-permissiveness" came into being, reached its height in the 1960s, and has lasted until now, but we are growing tired of it.*

'*The bursting of the bubble had to come. It was our first faltering attempt to come to terms with life in a pluralist society. We suddenly realised that we were no longer living in a world where there were commonly accepted standards of what was right and wrong or even of what was true or false. No one can say it was an ungenerous attempt. Let every minority, we said, have its platform. Let everybody choose his own life-style, and "do his own thing". We raised tolerance almost to the top of the league table of virtues.*

'*Societies can make worse choices than that, but then we made a serious mistake. We confused tolerance with neutrality.*

The so-called "silent majority" came into being, who lulled themselves into the belief that every point of view is only a point of view. We thought good sense would prevail in the end. We had forgotten the sort of society in which we are now living. There is no longer a normal standard accepted in our world against which everything else can be measured.'

The bishop's long-term answer is a life-style marked by personal discipline. Among the Archbishop's correspondents, however, were some to whom his first paragraph referred.

'Corporal punishment should be brought back for violence.'

'Two years' National Service should be compulsory from sixteen to eighteen. Why do other European countries have this and not us?'

'Bring back hanging for terrorism.'

There was a widely-expressed belief that violence and sex on television were in part to blame for it all. An old man, living in an area where *'the elderly are afraid to go out at night'* wrote *'Recent TV programmes on all stations call the police "pigs", even in so-called comedy series. In a BBC "Softly, Softly" programme they showed how easy it is for young hooligans to walk into a supermarket and place bombs amongst goods on the shelves and then threaten the manager to hand over the takings or they will go off when they are caught. When these hooligans see that our over-worked police are scorned and continually called "pigs" by the people who show these programmes, what respect can the young have for law and decency?'*

It must be some sort of a comment that a small convent school-girl in Worcester could end her very friendly letter to the Archbishop, *'Have you got a bodyguard?'*

Parental truancy

It is a striking fact that the Archbishop received many more letters referring to the effects of the absence from home of working mothers than about children who go wrong. The need for a parent to be home when children get back from school was far and away the most frequent suggestion of how to improve the quality of home and family life. This was sometimes linked with the assumption that mothers who go out to work '*are only out for more money*'.

Scores of letters revealed two class stereotypes that seemed to be believed implicitly. The first was that working-class mothers were doing it because they were greedy (there being several incomes coming into the home already). The second was that middle-class mothers did it as an assertion of Women's Lib, in order to fulfil their non-maternal, professional yearnings. Both, it was commonly stated, deprive the unemployed (especially the school-leaver never-yet-employed) of the jobs they should be holding down.

The problem with stereotypes, of course, is that they could often confuse the issue. A health visitor in Cornwall could write in International Women's Year, '*Why is not more emphasis put upon the greatest rôle she plays, that of motherhood, for truly to rear a child well is to surpass all other careers.*' It does not need much imagination to guess what response that would get in a group of university women, or of poor mums, and yet it points truthfully, and asks a question that cannot be avoided. In many of the discussion groups which have subsequently tackled the Archbishop's two questions, there has been a spread of interests and points of view in which some of these fixed stereotypes have come under serious challenge.

Some mothers do have to go to work in order that the family can make ends meet. Some wives ought to pursue a career, for their own sakes, and because they are good at it and the country needs their skills. Nevertheless, the Archbishop's letters are remarkable for the weight of testimony they offer on the other side.

'*I feel we have to strive to get mothers to accept that they are not strange in not wanting to go outside the home to work.*' (Essex)

'*Looking round our country today, it seems to me that what we need is not more women lorry-drivers, jockeys, stock-brokers (or even doctors and cabinet ministers), but simply more women who are prepared to devote their time, energies and talents to being good mothers. To recognise the equal importance of the male and female rôles is, in my opinion, to recognise the* true *equality of the sexes.*' (Monmouth)

The last word is from a juvenile court magistrate in the South. '*I am so glad you mentioned the family unit because in my work I see even in my rather rural area, the lack of the closely-knit family — doing things together, being together, and therefore giving the child a sense of security.*'

LOVE

Happy home life — this was the second main area of agreement in the letters — teaches and runs on love. Love — open relationships, perseverance towards real communication, willing the best for others.

A professional woman recently become a housewife and full-time mother again, wrote *'We really need a society in which people are more important than possessions. If more women, and young mothers in particular, could feel some sense of joy in giving up their jobs instead of feeling guilty that they are wasting their previous training etc., then they would have more time to love and enjoy their families. As God is love, then without love it is not surprising that children become delinquent and violent and involved in unhappy early marriages.'*

As a primary school headmistress in Somerset put it, *'More love is needed in the home: the cuddle on mother's lap is far better than the giving of an expensive toy or an overdose of TV.'*

If these are important basic needs of the young child, the need for the home to express love does not diminish with the years. A Methodist G.P. commented, *'I see a good deal of unhappiness which comes from the breakdown of relationships in the family, and also from the emotional confusion which stems from the devaluing of all our relationships in this so-called permissive (or perhaps more aptly termed apathetic) society.'*

A diocesan official in the South, who is a marriage guidance counsellor and also involved in many branches of social service, believed that *'you come back again and again to the failure in the home as the point where all the other battles are lost before they begin. It is no use expecting labour and management to discuss their differences creatively; or spokespeople for Women's Lib and "establishment" to accept one another's right to hold their own views;*

or any of a hundred and one other examples of communication breakdown, if in their own homes and the shelter of their own family, people's relationships have never developed, or have stayed snarled up.'

A minister's wife wondered *'what most of the activities of our congregations have to do with real education for life as most of us have to live it? If we were to start with the acceptance of the fact that most of the learning process happens pre-school (or doesn't happen), and that healthy people have to learn how to relate to others creatively (something that doesn't happen automatically), maybe we would concentrate much more on the home and family?'*

A Sussex family '(*harmoniously ecumenical — Church of Scotland, Congregational and Anglican!*)' wrote, '*A right attitude to the family can only come from a right attitude between the sexes. We have come to accept "permissiveness" as a sort of social evolution rather than as a deterioration.'* They went on to ask how the true meaning and importance of marriage could be restored. '*Too often a church or chapel wedding is little more than a social event with no religious follow-up.*' And, of course, more and more marriages are contracted now without a church service at all. And more and more break down. But love can be in and through all manner of apparent failure. '*By the way,*' wrote a divorced father in the Midlands, '*I am thirty-three and unemployed, and bring up four happy children. It is not money that has made them happy, it's LOVE.*'

Most examples were less fortunate. A lady in Essex worried '*about the break-up of so many marriages and the resultant emotionally insecure children. These children, I am afraid, are going to grow up to become disturbed personalities. Could we not point out with a louder voice the repercussions of such break-ups?'*

A Roman Catholic wife *'does not see how we shall get a return to family life with divorce so easy to get, and made so fashionable.'* She went on to say that the fact that *'Anglicans are not making a stand on divorce'* was one of her reasons for becoming a Catholic.

Are you watching Big Brother?

By far the most seriously felt threat to family life and to the stable development of loving human relationships, according to the evidence of the Archbishop's correspondence, was TV. Porn and the press got a look in, but it was television itself (all channels) which sustained the most concentrated attacks. Indeed, it is not exaggerating to say that many writers viewed the box in the sitting room as some sort of a Big Brother medium for persistent undermining of moral and religious scruples, a gigantic and devilish manipulation going well beyond '1984' and all that. Some saw this as a deliberately engineered plot, others as *'what's happened'*. Both groups felt impatient with, or embarrassed by, the others, but all agreed on the scapegoat itself.

'The box has taken over.'

'Up until recently we were able to select each programme in advance, or to switch off, but now with all these trailers or two minutes' snippets of forthcoming programmes wedged in between others, it is impossible to control just what comes flooding into our homes.'

'*Would you PLEASE, on behalf of all parents, (many of whom are really worried), try with all means possible to insist on good, clean, honest and decent standards in our media.*'

'*What about a real effort to let good news have a look in alongside the gloom and violence and despair in the news programmes?*'

There were three main areas which people felt certain needed challenging. The first was the very close tie-up between pressures on consumers to buy goods or services which they could well do without, and the life-style assumptions written into so much television. Many have got the message now that it is not only the commercials on one channel which sell things. The whole output of all channels is a powerful inducement to escalating demand.

'*Over the last thirty years we have learned that advertising can sell anything. Its most rewarding techniques have been the sale of sex and violence, with every home in the land bombarded from first thing in the morning to last thing at night seven days each week.*'

'*Brainwashing, on whatever subject, does rub off — usually on the basis of somebody somewhere selling something and lining the firm's pocket. It appeals, it is absorbed, and becomes accepted: it is necessary to have (as we say) possessions, sex, etc. Even if the not so young (such as me) get fed up to the teeth with the sound and the sight of too much too often, even these negative feelings are doing moral harm in the long run.*'

'*Horse-racing is good visual action, like soccer. But surely the encouragement to gambling which is so obviously part of it (let alone the extra boosts which ITV give even to this aspect) needs looking at?*'

'*So many ads tell you how easy it is to get money. All those clothes for only £5 a month, it says. Gone are the days, it seems, when you saved up the money to buy what you needed.*'

A school-girl comments, '*Television must take most of the blame for making people envious in the way they show quite ordinary people possessing these luxury items. I feel they would do more service to society if they showed the countless number of families, not only in this country, who find great happiness in a simple life with few possessions but living nearer to God.*'

The second area (and this was mentioned over and over again) was what is loosely called 'permissiveness'. Thousands wrote to say that they believed the week-in week-out portrayal of permissive relationships, bad language, and disregard for stabilising factors in society, *in our homes by a powerful medium of communication*, was dragging our country down. Television, by and large, was not seen to be on the side of making home and family life warm, human and genuinely personal. In terms of 'what sort of society do we want?' a majority of those who wrote wanted changes, maybe drastic changes, in the whole style and tone of TV.

An O.A.P. wanted '*the amount of sex, violence and obscene language used on TV and radio plays* banned' (and many others talked about censorship).

What in many ways was equally revealing in the letters was the experience people shared of being unable to get what they felt to be a personal and responsible answer from the media people about it all.

From Derby someone said, '*Anyone who attempts to*

stand up to them is made to look a fool by the media.' Many who wrote to the Archbishop had learned how difficult it is to get more than an acknowledgment from a producer ('*not all who have written agree with your point of view*'). Some had entered the lists alongside Mary Whitehouse. Many others were disquieted but felt unable to go public in that way. Reading again the hundreds of letters on this theme, one is struck by the immense frustration which they express, both with standards in the media, and with the inability of ordinary people to make any impression on those responsible for something that is bound to affect their children and their homes.

'*Those of us who are trying to bring up our children to have high moral standards feel we are battling against almost insurmountable odds,*' wrote a mother in Surrey.

This takes us back again to the Bishop of Dorking, of course. Another correspondent, himself in the media scene, wrote, '*Much as I have often to sympathise with what people say when they are complaining about something in a programme, the fact remains that these are usually very high-rating big-audience shows, which suggests that not everyone agrees with what they write. In fact, the "anti-permissives" are not always a majority among the post.*'

The third area of grave concern was crime and violence on TV. '*It's the criminal who gets all the publicity.*' '*Violence, crime and greed get so much publicity that one is led to think that these vices are the order of the day.*' And once again parents associated their difficulties in establishing stable guide-lines for their children, with all that was coming into the home by TV.

It is difficult to argue about this objectively. One writer deplored the following statement in a church magazine by the Rev. Paul Oestreicher, '*What about Mary Whitehouse's worries and those of the Festival of Light? I admire their critical attitude, because journalists shouldn't be allowed to get away with shoddy and dishonest programmes. Stern critics are often one's best friends. In press and TV there is a lot that's trivial and cheap. All the materialism and greed of our society is reflected and not just in advertising. But the puritan middle-class fears of Mrs. Whitehouse and her friends do nothing to enhance Christian values. Much of the real life drama they want to keep off the screen and out of print shows human beings wrestling seriously with themselves and the world. Sex, beautiful and not so beautiful, is too important to be turned into sweet romance. And violence is part of our sad reality. Yes, freedom is sometimes abused. We all abuse the freedom God gives us. Some bad programmes are the inevitable price we have to pay for the good ones.*'

The sense of frustration plus the genuineness of the concerns for the home and for our country in all this correspondence, cannot be ignored. When statements about '*indoctrination*' by '*powerful elements in the media*', '*the enemies of Christianity*', keep recurring, one has to ask whether this is only paranoia? Is it only the uneven adjustment of certain Christians to secular society over which they have no moral control? (reflected a little perhaps in the large number who urged the Archbishop to '*get the BBC to reintroduce Big Ben striking at nine p.m., so that the nation can have a daily 'minute' with God*').

Or is all this, deep down, something more than a

minority seeking to uphold crumbling traditions?
Could this reflect the truly human spirit, genuine in
its concern for the next generations? Since many of
the letters came from people disclaiming a Church
connection, at least this final question has to be faced.

CARING

The third area in which home and family life were
seen as being threatened today, was in caring and
practical concern for one another. There was a
great deal of interest in the letters in the ways in
which the welfare state works, and its effect on us all.
This was felt to have involved a subtly damaging
change in attitudes in the family and the local
community.

Some were deeply concerned about the gaps in
the present system, and rightly so. Deprived children
had a very vocal lobby. Families in the 'poverty
trap' (some of whom told their story to the Archbishop very movingly). The homeless. Those men-
tally ill who need not be in care if communities and
families and friends accepted again their traditional
role.

Many wrote from bitter experience of the 1930s,
and against a lifetime of hard struggle. None would
want to see again the deprivation of an earlier
generation. But these same people now questioned
the extent to which the pendulum had swung.

A lady of eighty, brought up in the East End, one

of a family of nine, '*remembered the unemployed marching through the streets. The much needed reform of trade unions was just beginning to be recognised, and I can remember my father saying that this was a good thing but that future generations would find this a stranglehold ... Greed and envy did not take precedence in the days of poverty. We were brought up to give and take and to be happy within the family. I have lived through three wars, two of them world wars, but today we are called upon to fight a more insidious foe, that of materialism and godlessness.*'

She went on, '*The welfare state has much to answer for. It has taken away that good old spirit of British independence and put in its place a grabbing attitude which considers the state to be responsible for his well-being. I have recently been in hospital for an operation for cataract and I was compelled to live on the state for a fortnight. I have nothing but praise for the treatment I received, but I feel that every patient should pay something. After all, we have to live when at home, and that expense ceases when in hospital. So many things to put right.*'

Or consider this plea from a family with no Church connection, who nevertheless wanted to tell the Archbishop how they felt when they heard what he said. They live in Cheshire.

'*My husband and I like so many others have worked long and hard (in a retail fruit business) to buy a house, furniture and a car, and have managed to do this with a measure of security. We wish to be self-reliant and do not want to be dependent on the state, nor do we want the state to take so great a proportion of our money in rates and taxes to decide for us what we shall have and not have. I believe that a more limited welfare state should exist only for those who are less fortunate, or handicapped etc. I may be wrong, but I think it weakens character when little by little our freedom of choice is taken from us.*

'*I came from a working-class background with honest and capable parents who never owed any money. We had no luxuries but we did have time to go family walks, piano evenings, cards, friends, etc.*'

There were many others who wrote in similar vein. From Nottingham, '*I am a middle-aged woman, wife of a lower-paid worker. We have struggled through the years to buy our own house, old though it may be. We have asked for nothing. We only had one child, so no child allowance. What we have achieved we did ourselves. When we look round and see all the handouts people are getting from this welfare state, we sometimes feel so sad that what should be a wonderful thing has really turned out to sap the goodness and initiative from so many of our people.*'

From another part of the country, and another background, a correspondent put the blame for '*undermining the family*' on to this same '*growing assumption by the state of functions which used to be performed by members of the family. The care of the aged, the upbringing of children, for example, is becoming more and more impersonal as the state increasingly takes over from private individuals. The reverse of this process would strengthen family ties.*'

A couple in Hereford wanted '*the emphasis moved away from impersonal institutions to supportive activities in the welfare area.*' (going on to say this made economic sense very often, too). '*We do not pretend that the family unit can solve all the individual's problems and, indeed, recognise that there are whole families that need outside help.*

Nevertheless, giving and sharing within the family can lift the whole level at which life is lived. It offers scope for the individual to count.'

It is very significant that so often those who wrote wanted to link the welfare state and the quality of family life. Someone who had been in Canada at the time of the 'Call' wrote subsequently about a Provincial consultation in British Columbia on the whole range of issues which arise here. Jointly sponsored by the Legislature and the churches working ecumenically, a detailed programme of national and local-level discussion was happening. The aim was to discover the truly human lines of demarcation between family and state responsibility (a 'mixed family economy'), and to come, as a sizeable community, to considered views on 'what sort of a society do we want to be' in this sector of life.

What the Archbishop's correspondence seemed to suggest very strongly was that many would be encouraged to see such a consultation set up here. It might be on the basis of 'The Family Matters', starting there for once, rather than happening to come into the purview of the broadcasting enquiry, or a social benefits enquiry, or a housing enquiry.

No one *planned* the series of pressures on home and family to which this chapter has referred. The fear behind many letters has been that without a concerted effort now, these may succeed in finally breaking down the backbone of stable community.

Questions

1. What do you see as the pros and cons of mothers going out to work?
2. Can a family be united without agreeing together on the limits they will place on TV in the home?
3. Did you make sense of Paul Oestreicher's statement on page 67, '*Some bad programmes are the inevitable price we have to pay for the good ones.*' What do you yourself accept as the cost of being part of a secular society?
4. What has most of what church congregations now spend their time on got to do with effective education for life? (p. 62)
5. Where would you want to see the welfare state extended and where contracted? If this involves 'means tests' how could this be done more humanly and acceptably than hitherto?
6. If there were a national consultation on the family, what factors would you want it to consider?

4

Good Work Matters

His THIRD STATEMENT took the Archbishop right into the political and economic arena. In Biblical terms, this is where prophets function. A school-teacher in Hull reported how *'in teaching girls of twelve to thirteen about the prophets and most recently about Amos, Hosea and Micah, the class and I came to the conclusion that we needed a prophet just as much today. Then your message came and we decided that prophecy was not dead after all.'* She shared something of their further discussion, and then concluded, *'I sincerely hope some ways can be found to achieve your ends, but as one child said, "They wouldn't listen to Amos, would they?"'*

What the Archbishop had said was straight to the point. **'A good day's work for a fair day's pay' isn't a bad motto for worker *and* for management. But pay isn't everything. "Each for himself and the devil take the hindmost" makes for chaos. Guzzling doesn't satisfy. Grabbing and getting is a poor creed. Envy is a cancer. Sacrifice is an unpopular word; discipline even more so. But without sacrifice, without disci-**

**pline, and without a sense of responsibility at
the heart of our society, we're likely to perish.
A bit of hardship hurts none of us. Can you
deny it? We're growing soft!'**

How all this was heard makes a fascinating study of
communication in the TV age. Remember it was the
press conference at which these words were said which
launched the 'Call' on radio, TV and in the papers.

There were those who dismissed it angrily as
naive, middle-class backing-the-bosses union-bashing.
'*Today's version of the Protestant work ethic.*' The phrase
'*and* for management' failed to register. A correspondent noted how in one of the TV broadcasts with
the Archbishop, '*people latched on to and rejected the idea
of self-denial by the workers*'. Someone recently made
redundant wrote '*as one who is at present out of work, in
my opinion as a result of people making money their priority
to an excessive degree*'.

A housewife in Essex picked out the theme of '*the
leaders of the trade unions seeing the error of their ways and
so helping their men to be more unselfish in their demands*'.
Another, in East Anglia, an ex-civil servant, recalled
unofficial strike pickets stopping her and some friends
from carrying on working. '*Quite a few, on questioning,
admitted they only went on strike because the others did.*'

Others were perhaps more ready to see another
side to it all. A Northern worker explained, '*If a
person in industry puts his priorities in the right order at
present, he will arouse the antipathy of his colleagues
because of the quality and quantity of his work. He will
arouse the antagonism of the unions if in serving his
conscience he refuses to take part in coercion, restrictive*

practices or stoppages. He will arouse the antagonism of management when he refuses to accept purely commercial values (profit before people, profit before purpose, profit before benefit to society). His forbearance and tolerance will be misconstrued by many of his colleagues and managers as weakness or ingratiation.'

A substantial number heard the Archbishop and wondered why he had not specifically *'addressed his remarks to those responsible — mainly — those leaders of trade unions who are avowed communists. Many workers are forced to belong to trade unions in order to retain, or obtain, employment — completely against their wishes.'* That comment came from a lady in Kent, but similar references to the *'infiltration of labour and of our schools and of the whole of society by the communists'* were made by very many.

But the correspondence was far from one-sided. From the South Coast a company secretary wrote, *'I approve and support in principle your call for a less selfish way of life, but you should address your remarks more specifically to the wealthy and privileged. I live among ordinary citizens. Speaking for them, I think it is hypocrisy for so-called leaders to ask them to make sacrifices for the country. I read recently of heads of industry receiving golden handshakes from £300,000 to £30,000, in some cases for sitting on boards of directors for periods of little more than ten months. The ordinary working person would be paid just redundancy pay. How can anyone call upon the average working person to make sacrifices in the face of these ridiculous parting gifts? One in a TV interview was asked what he proposed to do now, and replied that he was going to take a "well-earned holiday". I suppose that was his*

*idea of a sacrifice! Let us attack the position of the wealthy,
the speculator, etc. rather than the trade unionist, the worker
or ordinary person who has little or no room to manoeuvre.*'

Others advised the Archbishop to look to White-
hall and Westminster for the main offenders. A
Londoner wrote, '*You have addressed us, the general
public, instead of the government. We keep hearing the
country is broke. Only £6 for increases, the country can't
afford more. So what happens? To prove to us that the
country is not able to pay more, they give China ten million
pounds . . .*' (and a whole list of other extraordinary
expenditure follows). From Norfolk came an O.A.P's
plea to the Archbishop to address his comments to
the government first. '*Let Mr. Wilson and co. show a
good example, let* them *stop this* "grabbing" *to which you
refer, let* them *give us all an incentive. The British people
do not mind hard work or hardship; that has been proven,
but they hate being stifled.*'

A vicar's wife felt that ' "*a fair day's work for a fair
day's pay*" *must be set within a context in which we can
believe (which we can't at present) in the right stewardship
of* our *money by those in power*'.

Someone else felt justified in pointing a formal
parallel between the Archbishop's 'Call' ('*void of
social* content') and the sort of calls put out by the
German Christian movement in Hitler's Reich.

The Bishop of Southwark

Then, of course, the Bishop of Southwark wrote his
article in the *Morning Star*. As this was taken up by

all the media the same day, it brought enormous fresh interest to the 'Call'. It also resulted in a fresh deluge of letters to Lambeth, many of them copies of letters sent directly to the Bishop.

Dr. Mervyn Stockwood had basically been critical of the Archbishop's emphasis on the responsibility of the individual. Since for the most part the individual, particularly the worker, had very little room to manoeuvre, and was almost entirely conditioned by his environment within the system we are committed to in the Western democracies, the Bishop felt the 'Call' should have been an attack upon the system itself.

That was a point that *had* to be made in the debate the 'Call' had brought into focus. Others had already been making it in the correspondence. The radical questioning of our social, political and economic systems was to be a part of the various study programmes that would be prepared in different parts of the country in response to the 'Call'.

What riled great numbers of correspondents was what they saw as the Bishop's 'disloyalty'. That point can be argued various ways. As the Archbishop himself said when addressing General Synod in February 1976, '*A certain amount of controversy has been engendered*, and that is all to the good, *for one of the prime reasons for the Call was to open up a debate on matters of serious concern.*'

Worse, in many people's view, was that the Bishop of Southwark should use a communist daily in which to publicise his reaction to the Archbishop. His own defence to this criticism was that since highly critical remarks had already appeared in the *Morning Star*, a more balanced statement (nevertheless reflecting some of the views of the readers) would help rather than hinder.

Finally, and at this point maybe the Bishop had been carried away by his own enthusiasms, he had stated that under a truly socialist system, pornography and the other evils of London's West End would be cleared up overnight. This statement, bald and unqualified, was of course taken up in headlines and interviews by the media. It was all too easy to imply that a diocesan Bishop had publicly rejected the Archbishop and had advocated a communist takeover. As has been seen before, there already existed an undercurrent of suspicion that we were in process of being taken over anyway, so the furore Bishop Stockwood's words caused was predictable.

Two good points and one bad one emerged after the shouting died down. First, people had been made to think about the Archbishop's two questions in ways they might not otherwise have done. A correspondent in North London said frankly, '*the fact that the Bishop attacks it tells me yours was a good and important challenge. Therefore, I shall now study what you said in detail, having regarded it as merely of passing interest when you made your statement.*'

Secondly, there was a very strong case to be made in stressing what the Gospels may have to say to the existing structures of our society, and this cannot be wholly implied in statements about personal responsibility. Preaching subsequently in his old church, Great St. Mary's, in Cambridge, the Bishop was to

say of Christ as he is described in the words of the
Magnificat,

' *"He scatters the proud in the imagination of their
hearts" — that is moral change. When Christ is King he
"puts down the mighty and exalts the humble" — that is
social change. When Christ is King, he "fills the hungry
with good things, and sends the rich empty away" — and
that is economic change ... The words of the Magnificat
spell out not a programme, but an attitude towards a programme. It is not the function of Christians, as such, to
draw up any itemised programme. What we can do is to
give people an approach which is based on Scripture. Now I
have no doubt that if the Church is to influence contemporary
society, we have got to move along these three lines of
change — moral, and social and economic.*'

The third outcome of the Bishop's intervention, on
the negative side, was that for a space most of the
argument narrowed to pro- or anti-communism.
Many wanted to identify the Archbishop's 'other
enemy at the gates today' as communism in any
case, and the Bishop had played into their hands.

Soon after the 'Call' the Archbishop was in Nairobi
for the Assembly of the World Council of Churches.
In an interesting comment on the debate, as it was
then developing in Britain, a discerning fellow-
participant could say of this Assembly, '*From Uppsala
in 1967 there came a great thrusting word and the word was
justice. From Nairobi I do not think it was a word as
simple, direct and penetrating as that. To some extent this
may be a very good thing. It means that some of the com-
plexities of these problems of our world was more fully
recognised.*' Kenneth Slack, the Director of Christian

Aid: '*It means again a deeper recognition that our pro-foundest problem is the evil of the human heart and not just the evil of the structures that perpetuate and embody injustice.*'

Eight pointers

The dust soon settled. Most people realised that the Archbishop's statement had not been '*incredibly naive*' but had been a media presentation to get a discussion going. From the first few months of that discussion eight closely connected themes emerged.

I. PEOPLE NEED TO WORK

A seventy-year-old Londoner, life-long trade unionist, wrote, '*I have been out of work, and know how demoralising it is to walk around looking for work.*'

This is not so much a question of getting money to support oneself and the family. There have been times when we could be excused for thinking this was the point. More adequate social benefits have made it easier to see now the underlying and even more important factors to which this correspondent was pointing.

Expanding on it himself, three weeks after the 'Call', the Archbishop said, '*In order to be fully human a man needs to work, to be part of a creative process, and to know that he is doing a job that is worthwhile. In the doing of that job lies a large part of his dignity as a person.*'

Many of those who wrote about the need for wives

to concentrate on the family rather than going out to work if there was no unavoidable economic reason, had this in mind too.

'Could Women's Institutes and Young Wives' Groups not stress as a sacrifice that mothers who do not actually need extra money, expend their energies in making real homes for their husbands and children. This would leave jobs free, e.g. for teenagers leaving school, and thus reducing unemployment.'

As the Archbishop has constantly underlined, if man as man is made for creative activity, then our first priority towards one another in any society is to pay the price of helping all our fellow men to have a job. This applies with particular force to those who have never worked before.

'Unemployment, and especially the unemployment of the school-leaver, is one of our greatest enemies. Each successive government addresses itself to the problem and finds the solution elusive. What worse fate can await an adolescent than to go out into a world which cannot employ him?'

A retired worker who had been through it for himself, commented, *'It is not right when so many of them have passed their exams, that they have to face a start in life just as bad and harmful as we did in the 1920s and 1930s.'* And a lady in Sussex added, *'What is going to happen to them through hours of idleness and boredom at a time of life that they should be working hard?'*

The Archbishop proposed one first-aid measure, which has subsequently been taken up under existing statutory provisions, *'Could not government, central and local, aided by trade unions, colleges, Rotarians and so on, organise an environmental "spring clean" of our cities and*

countryside, and pay the youngsters thus employed a re-
muneration slightly higher than that which they would
receive through public assistance?'

2. WORK MUST MEAN SOMETHING

'It is not only the production-line where boredom can set
in. Office-work is boring too. The difference is that in an
office you can disappear for a while, or gossip, or make a
long private phone-call, and it will not notice.'

If honest people can write like that, then there is
a lot of rethinking to be done about the sort of work
we set each other to do. The size of work-unit, the
working conditions themselves, the extent to which
people feel they are participating in creating a worthwhile product, and are being rewarded for success
along the way; all these factors matter. It is not
enough to talk about attitudes to work as if there were
no questions to be asked about the jobs we do, and
the circumstances in which we have to do them.

Having said that, however, it has to be reported
that many of the Archbishop's correspondents did
raise the matter of attitudes.

A Port Talbot steel-worker wrote, *'May I try to*
stress what I consider a very important aspect of religion, our
attitude to work. After fifty years spent in the metal
industries, I retired after long hours and little pay, but
proud and happy to enjoy the greatest reward — the know-
ledge of having tried to perform my humble duties not only
to the best of my ability, but progressively. I was brought up
to believe work well done was an elementary but basic
ingredient of religion.'

This correspondent recalled Chesterton's thought, *'If the people of Pimlico loved Pimlico as a mother loves her children, Pimlico in no time would be fairer than Florence'*, and also *'what was said of Amiel, "He went to his desk as to an altar"'*.

Several correspondents quoted versions of the story of the men working on the construction of St. Paul's Cathedral. When asked what they were doing, one replied, 'Moving rubbish'. Another said, 'Earning a wage to keep the family going.' A third replied, 'Helping Sir Christopher to build a cathedral.'

There is a real confusion in people's mind and experience of all this, reflected in the letters. A Southend housewife could write, *'Remuneration is not all important, but the privilege of serving other people is far more important, and the fact that one's particular job of work is doing just that, is something to be proud of and grateful for.'* On the other hand, a social worker in the North was *'very concerned about the attitude of many of the young qualified social workers today who are more interested in their own salaries and homes than with the needs of their clients. The same attitude is widespread in other professions among the newly qualified, who consider that our generation were stupid to work in the way we did.'*

Something has gone seriously wrong with society over a long period when job-satisfaction is apparently denied to so many. Some said this was built in to the capitalist system, so change the system. Others said reform the system wherever you can.

A self-confessed idealist wrote, *'The greatest failing in a society is to condemn its members to boredom. The ideal society would aim at variety, not "one man, one job". We should all be Jacks of all trades. This would involve the end of trade union separatism. The factory worker should be capable of a score of jobs and do them. . . . The great lie of the twentieth century is that God made all men equal. The great truth which needs to be proclaimed is that God made all men different. If each cultivates his talents and donates them to society, society will be richer, and men in it happier.'*

How to translate ideals into practical next steps? This is the crunch question. Meanwhile let idealism speak again, in the words of an eleven-year-old school-girl, *'When I get older and get a job I am going to be one of the people who work most of the time like the nurses and doctors in hospitals. Sometimes they work all night and day and don't get a rest.'*

3. WORK PATTERNS ARE SHIFTING

'I am just a widow who runs a fifty acre farm, and for me the great question is can capitalism work *when challenged by socialism. The amassing of capital presupposes a class willing to create wealth by taking a smaller proportion of the cake.* Now this class is in revolt . . . *The paramount ethic of capitalism today is* profit. *If men and the interests and wholesome needs of men are sacrificed to this ethic, we are in trouble. Automation, speculation in currency, replacing men with machines, and doing nothing to help them keep self-respect, this too is chaos. The upper- and middle-classes in so far as they have reaped the benefits have been unaware of this.'*

It may be that the public are more ready to face and talk about changing work patterns as they dictate our future, than the politicians and leaders of labour and industry seem to imagine. At the Lord Mayor's Banquet, several weeks after the 'Call', the Archbishop pleaded for the setting up of a series of think-tanks for long-term discussion. One of the topics he wanted to see treated was this: '*How do we re-gear our education programme so as to prepare our young people for a life no longer dominated by long working hours? How do we train them for the creative use of that leisure which will constitute a major part of their lives as automation increasingly takes over?*'

From Bradford came a long letter headed 'Full Employment'. It went to the heart of our dilemma. '*Automation is a common word, meaning that automatic machines controlled by press buttons now produce many times the quantity of goods formerly produced by many men. Cybernation is a later development meaning that at the end of a process the automatic machines now do the button-pressing for the next stage themselves, and men are now not needed even for that. In agriculture, seed is sown by seed-drilling machines, and the harvest of cereals is gathered by combine-harvesters, and the crops dried by mechanical driers. A greater abundance of food is being produced by fewer and fewer men. The trend of industry and agriculture is not only continuing inexorably in that direction, but the pace of its acceleration is increasing. And yet the slogan of the governments, the industrialists, and the trade unions, is "Full Employment". It is preposterous.*'

Thus, the letter goes on to argue, '*the principal cause of unemployment is redundancy. Men are not wanted to produce the goods, machines can do it. When men cease work, the production of goods, the country's total output, does not diminish. On the contrary, it increases.*'

In industry after industry (and increasing too in banking and commerce, as computers are improved) this process seems inexorable. The logic seems simple enough. The working week (since man must work, for reasons we have already looked at), will have to be constantly reduced in line with reducing needs for the human presence at work. Since man needs to work, we must share around fairly what work has to be done, and ask radical questions about what new forms of creative effort we can discover.

But if that is to be anything like practical politics, then the whole 'rewards' system (wages, salaries, productivity deals, career structures, job-satisfaction) has to be looked at again almost from scratch. The correspondent from Bradford felt that this hinged upon '*a complete re-think of the present methods of creating and issuing new money. The money supply needs to be balanced with the value of production,*' and thereafter the money '*would have to be distributed with reasonable equity to all the country's citizens. Only thus can unemployment be welcome as paid leisure.*'

Closely in line with this, a correspondent from Edinburgh raised the question of long periods of paid absence from work. '*The introducing of sabbatical years into working lives may appear to conflict with your "Appeal". But both are aimed at improving the quality of life rather than seeking to raise the standard of living.*' He went on to quote a *Guardian* article by Walter Chamberlain (August 28th, 1975) in which there had been set out a drastic suggestion for this sort of contribution to a society that was coming to terms with automation. How would people use such a year? They would be free to do as they wished, only provided it was not working in their usual trade. Some would study, or re-train. Others would travel, or undertake voluntary service, or concentrate on a sport. At the end of the year they would be absolutely guaranteed their job back if they wished to return to it. He concluded, *'Could the country afford to lose such a large proportion of its labour force? Consider the alternatives, an overburdened educational system, inefficient industries trying to stretch work out, people frantically trying to adjust their budgets when told they must retire earlier, lengthening dole and bankruptcy queues and loss of confidence in the ability of a democratic government to solve the problem.'*

Other proposals along similar lines have included longer holidays during working years, more one-day public holidays, fiscal encouragement for firms to experiment in job enrichment, worker participation, and much greater use of part-time labour (male and female).

Here was evidence that numbers of people are prepared to bring out into the open questions which underlie the changing work-pattern which society is experiencing today.

If we do not give them urgent consideration, then are we not wide open, as we have already seen in other contexts, to some other sort of revolution or take-over? The logic of Western technocratic man's success seems to be that he must now undertake the one revolution or face the likelihood of the other.

4. REWARDS MUST NOT VARY SO MUCH IF OUR SOCIETY IS TO *FEEL* FAIR

I have already quoted letters which make this point. The expectations of a 'golden hand-shake' in the boardroom as against minimum redundancy pay from the shop-floor does not go unnoticed. Nor, unfortunately for faith in the integrity of our legislators, did their latest pay rise prior to the imposition of the £6 a week limit. Large numbers of letters raised this. Correspondents found it extremely difficult to set M.P.s' action into the context of '*they had not had a rise for x years*' when constraint was being urged on others. A worker in the Midlands commented '*If the £6 limit had been started by the M.P.s at the time it was started, the country as a whole would have responded wholeheartedly.*'

As with the previous section, it seems here that we are faced with two alternatives by way of radical change. The one challenge is already with us. A teacher in Somerset wrote, '*I am finding more and more people are doing all they can to provide us with a generation of egalitarians, based on the premise that it is wrong for anybody to be better housed, better fed, better educated and better provided with the material things of life, than anybody else.*'

A good many wrote to the Archbishop saying they refused to listen to anything he said about sacrifice, because he lived in a palace and had a big salary. Often they linked the other bishops and the Royal Family with this. (We come back to this in detail in another chapter.)

It is not enough to argue this one in personal terms, and the attempt so to do seems fore-doomed not to be heard. When the Archbishop spoke at the 1975 Lord Mayor's Banquet, for example, he said *'It is generally recognised that one of the root causes of juvenile delinquency and violence is bad housing. Are there not many in Britain today who would be happy to accept a cut in their salaries if the money so saved could provide capital sums for renovating run-down property which would increase housing and encourage local employment? Is it starry-eyed to think that many people earning, say, £6,000 p.a. would accept a five per cent cut, those over £10,000 p.a. a ten per cent cut, and so on up the scale? A certain amount of organisation would be called for, but it is not beyond the wit of man to set such a plan going.'*

So far as I know, there was a nil response. Nevertheless the letters made it obvious that until there is some voluntary or imposed limitation on upper limits of remuneration, i.e. a determined effort at reducing the overal differential between 'top' and 'bottom' scales of pay, our society cannot feel anything but selfish, and calls to sacrifice will go on being heard in terms of class distinction.

Moreover, if the one self-imposed voluntary change does not happen, then additional fuel is being offered to the fire of the other revolution already looked at in the previous section. In our present attempts to preserve a 'mixed economy' (capitalist-socialist), one of the nettles we seem incapable of grasping is the way top levels of salary in nationalised industries have to bear a relationship to those pertaining outside. It is not a matter that can be dealt with solely by taxation. If ninety-five per cent of increases above a certain figure is taken in taxation, this merely dictates the gigantic size of any salary or increase likely to be expected above that figure, whether in the private or state sectors. How long do we need to go on as if there was nothing anyone could do about it?

A number of the Archbishop's correspondents were asking whether, if there is the will to change before the change is done for us, there could not be a commitment by all sections of society to a reduction in overall differential, maybe working on this over a decade, within some planned programme. The Archbishop's first question, 'What sort of a society do we want?' is bound to open up this sort of radical re-think. Some of the groups are already discussing this issue.

5. WE CANNOT LIMIT OUR RE-THINK TO UK FACTORS ONLY

At the end of his paragraph on a voluntary pay cut for the over-£6,000 p.a. people, the Archbishop fired another shot at the Lord Mayor's Banquet. '*All the while there is the third world knocking at our doors. Constant pressure should be brought to bear for the increase of foreign aid, and especially for the proposed World Agricultural Fund.*'

A Hertfordshire correspondent queried whether '*it is right to couch "the debate" in national terms? From history it seems invariably true that the betterment of one's national position in any respect is either to the neglect or bringing down of another nation. Should a Christian not insist that the "debate" is supra-national?*'

Linking this same thought with wider ecological considerations, a correspondent from Glasgow suggested, '*A moderation of our material demands, and a reassessment of our relationship with God and one another both nationally and internationally is surely indicated, for our total well-being? Also a more tender appreciation of Mother Earth?*'

John Lawrence, in his S.P.C.K. paperback *Take Hold of Change*, and Charles Elliott in his *Inflation and the Compromised Church* (Christian Journals Ltd., Belfast) were among those whose publications took up this theme in the months following the 'Call'.

6. WE NEED A NEW SOCIAL CONTRACT

In the light of all this, many correspondents wanted to plead for a clean slate, a new start, a fresh beginning (not always accepting the fact that even in the extreme situation of a revolution the slate is never wiped quite clean, and that in less drastic changes the room for manoeuvre is seldom as great as it appears).

'Action '75' had as one of its statements '*We recognise that the polarisation of the nation into irreconcilable groups is a condition that must be corrected. The failure of the various groupings among the population to trust or even understand any other section of the community is a basic cause of the nation's problems. We will therefore work to cure division, mistrust, hatred and indifference, whatever the cause.*'

Painful though it is, we do well to look at the nature of those divisions as they are expressed in the Archbishop's letters.

From the Thames Valley came a forthright, '*I feel compelled to respond to your courageous and relevant challenge to the silent majority, who are sick and tired of the cynical hypocrisy of the politicians of both parties.*

'*In 1945 the nation gave a huge majority to the socialist party to build a new Britain with equal opportunities for all. That trust was betrayed, and class divisions which the war had largely dissipated were re-established and encouraged. The welfare state, a concept that was intended to prevent suffering and need, was allowed, by pandering to impractical "do-gooders" and by manipulation to bribe electors with something — even everything — for nothing, to degenerate into a wasteful, inefficient, and basically unfair system.*

The huge majority who work hard and do their best are penalised, heavily taxed and vilified in order to support large numbers of idlers and scroungers. Now we all feel a kind of despair and tend to join the "take all, give the minimum" brigade.

We want a fair society, a new sense of pride in our nation and in the way we do our work. The nationalised industries must be something we treasure, efficient, cheap, and the envy of the world, not, as now, bankrupt.'

Another correspondent wrote, '*The politics of envy and greed must go — and if the two-party system cannot achieve that, then the people must be given the opportunity to vote, not for a party, not for an individual, but for principles and policies.*'

A seventy-two-year-old ex-bus driver believed '*if we were all working as a team, we could soon get this mess put right*', but felt it would need a new look at the power of the unions and at some of the social effects of the welfare state. '*The effort would be worth making, for we could not drift on as we had been doing.*'

A clergyman in the Midlands, with a glance back at how '*the Victorian middle-class tended to transform everything* (*the earth, property, the creations of men, men themselves*) *into objects of domination*'; a process of oppression he now saw repeated by some of the stronger unions, had his own vision of a new social contract.

'*I want a clear-sighted, accepting, sharing, constructive society and would look to our political, social and religious structures for signs of its realisation. However so much of our debate in this country is characterised by perpetual conflict in which scorn, mockery and invective are acceptable weapons. This institutionalised violence of political, social and religious scorn is sterile, out-moded, puerile and de-humanising. There is a better way — the way of Jesus Christ — the way of love: "I say this to you who are listening: Love your enemies, do good to those who hate you, bless those who curse you, pray for those who treat you badly."*

'*In an oppressive situation love is not possible. Only by abolishing the situation of oppression is it possible to restore love.* Only if the oppressed truly loves the oppressor and wants the best for him can both find liberation. This is the mark of the Christian revolutionary. *That this is our Christian vocation is indicated by the accusation hurled at Paul and Silas — "The people who have turned the world upside down have come here now."* '

7. WE NEED TO LOOK AGAIN AT THE SCALE OF THINGS

One of the points the Archbishop had stressed was the need for the individual to count himself in on local action. A widow now in Cambridgeshire wrote in response, '*Being one of a family of miners, including my late husband, I know from experience, both in that industry and in the B.S.C. which my husband joined after twenty-seven years in mining, it is the apathetic attitude of some; many people just do not attend their union meetings, with the results we are seeing today.*'

Even in the months since that was written there have been signs of change in that, of course. Perhaps this does reflect an awakening to the fact that the national-level people we see on the box each evening only hold their power, influence and responsibilities because ordinary people have at some point said so.

A young father, a worker in the Midlands, said, '*I may have seemed to be blaming others in what I have written, but I am not blameless. For one thing I have been one of the apathetic majority in my own T.U. branch. It is my intention to rectify this.*'

But it is not only trade union democracy that is at stake in this question of scale, local participation, and 'opting in'. The size of work-units, to which we referred earlier; the question of worker-participation in management and decision-making within a factory; the very processes of parliamentary voting (about which several correspondents wrote in detail), all are involved. If we are to face the dragon of size, and the fear it has engendered, almost inhibiting action of any sort, we have to learn to 'think big and act small'.

8. AND ALL THIS CALLS FOR A NEW STYLE EDUCATION FOR LIFE

Once you start to think in change terms, every facet of life becomes involved. Where education is concerned, nostalgia is clearly not enough, although there was plenty of it in the Archbishop's post-bag.

'*Years ago the Ten Commandments were taught and regularly repeated in day schools and Sunday Schools. Surely these are basic rules by which the whole community would benefit?*'

'*Every child should learn to appreciate the marvel of the creation of the universe out of the thought of God by the vibration of the power of his voice. There should be discussions on the Beatitudes, the Ten Commandments should be repeated and discussed at the beginning of every term.*'

'*What hope have we of bringing our semi-pagan nation back to a belief in God as long as our political rulers continue to play the fool with education (the very foundation of a nation's character)?*'

If the Ten Commandments were mentioned by hundreds of correspondents, there were not lacking those who were for getting rid of the last vestiges of 'religious influence' in the schools. '*I persist in my demand,*' said one, '*for a non-religious moral education course in state schools*', and guessed that the next time the issue came up for parliamentary debate there was a distinct possibility that even the 'moral education' baby would be thrown out with the R.E. 'bathwater'.

But important though these issues were, were they in fact where the 'education for life' question stood? Looking first at life as it must be in the later years of this century, leisure-dominated, reflecting the outcome of the size debate for better or for worse, coming to grips with the place of the electronic media in society, what might education be like?

Such questions revealed the sterility and pointlessness of large areas of current discussion and hostility.

A teacher in Birmingham wrote, '*After thirty years experience I am appalled at the way our educational system is declining in standards. All kinds of half-baked schemes are brought in unproven. I accept that we must have change, but wisdom calls for new ideas to be tested before being compulsorily brought in. The call for the abolition of examinations; mixed ability teaching; comprehensive schools, etc. — may or may not be good, but they need testing first on a small scale.*'

If those questions arose against yesterday's problems, what of tomorrow's? '*How do we train our young people for the creative use of that leisure which will constitute a major part of their lives?*' the Archbishop asked. Can we even enter this sphere of questioning without careful consideration of 'baby' and 'bathwater' — religious and moral education in the schools — since creativity, self-discipline and a sense of purpose to sustain them, are all part of that integration of personality which Christianity is about?

Questions

1. It often happens that those who enjoy their work most are also well paid for it. Do you feel that 'job satisfaction' should be regarded as part of the reward for the job, and salaries adjusted accordingly?

2. Where does automation touch your life? At work, at home, in leisure activities? Do you accept the fact that there is less 'work' to be shared round now? Do you think we can reshape society to cope with this?

3. If we were going to reduce the gap between the highest and lowest pay scales in a fair society, what might the difference be?

4. Discuss some of the differences there would have to be in our system of schooling if we took seriously the points raised in this chapter.

5. List some of the change-points suggested here as alternatives to another sort of revolution. How do you react in looking at them all on one sheet of paper?

6. At what one, or two, points can you see where a beginning could be made?

5

The Other Fellow Matters

'I believe the only creed that makes sense is:-
God first —
Others next —
Self last.
I see this worked out in the person and teaching
of Jesus Christ. He has shown us the way —
He gives us the power to follow it. And this is
where prayer comes in.'

In many of the Archbishop's letters there were
expressions of appalled concern for what people felt
to be the decadence of Britain today. This was the
background against which Dr. Coggan was heard
appealing for a return to religious standards and
morality. It is worth reading how people wrote of
the state and needs of their country.

After thirty years in Africa, and now retired here,
a correspondent recalled '*a gracious land*', but now found
'*values accepted here, habits, almost customs, tolerated, that
no African friend or worker would tolerate. Soft? Perhaps
not, but grown lazy, ill-bred, prepared to be supported
morally and financially by others, and discontented as well.*'

From four years in Pakistan, a lady wrote, '*I have been conscious since my return of the emphasis on materialism*'. Others referred to '*lack of discipline*', '*irresponsibility*', '*too much lightheartedness concerning immorality*', '*decay from within, hastened by attacks, some extremely subtle, upon authority*', '*the slide of a law-abiding, moral, Christian country into a pagan, permissive ruin*'.

This sort of comment was not from one age group only, nor from Church people only. A young housewife in the North wanted the Archbishop '*to make our politicians realise that decent people are in despair—that the way of life in this country has so deteriorated that no one knows where or who to turn to*'. An older mother from Gloucestershire expressed her despair like this: '*How can one "turn the clock back" as it were, so that self-discipline and hard work become "fashionable" instead of insistence on one's rights and preferring to be a passenger in society? So often Christianity seems to be regarded as an anachronism; Christians as irrelevant to social and political debate; the desire for a return to virtue and a proper distinction between right and wrong as some freakish reactionarism not yet abreast of the new liberalism.*'

A Northumberland correspondent hoped the Archbishop's words would be heeded '*both by those attempting to destroy our standards, and also by those (myself among them) who are possibly unwittingly and unwillingly finding that our own standards are beginning to fall*'.

Inevitably among the letters were some which attributed '*our decline*' to comparatively unsuspected causes, like the fluoridation of water-supplies or the factory-farming of chickens and livestock. A retired teacher of a social science curriculum saw the danger focused in the take-over of such teaching by '*an exaggerated and greedy intellectualism which became a new indoctrination*'.

A Welsh writer pointed again at the deeply resented differentials question which divided the nation, '*The One O'clock News today began with your statement — and ended with some Lord and Lady paying over £1300 for an overnight trip to Bahrein on the Concorde. They have nothing to envy, to turn away from materialism and return to a more spiritual way of life. Half that fare on Concorde could prevent a home, a son and mother, from all kinds of decay (bricks, wood, mortar and spiritual).*' There was the sense of an 'unfair' society, put very pointedly.

But of all the causes taken up in this correspondence, abortion received far and away the greatest attention. Thousands wrote because they could not see how our land could again become a place where 'the other fellow (or girl) matters' whilst this denial of the very principle itself was on the statute book. A district nurse, midwife and health visitor wrote, '*We appear to be heading for a society of organised misery — for isn't the sanctity of marriage ridiculed, infidelity flaunted, and promiscuity not only encouraged but the STATE almost insists that it be the daily diet for our young teenagers; at the same time making provision that if they do not welcome the end-product, 170,000 abortions can be arranged and paid for by the state in one year?*'

It was obvious that Roman Catholics were particularly vocal on this issue, but it would be a total misunderstanding to imagine that only R.C. opinion is outraged by the abortion laws. Many families of

all backgrounds see this the same way, and find the
Home Secretary's 'civilised society' ideals horrifying
in practice. It is not only the middle-aged or the
elderly who saw things that way, and wrote of their
sense of outrage.

A twenty-five-year-old student nurse asked, *'Why
do we always look for the easy way out of things (permissiveness, punishments, abortion on demand)? Why are
we brought up without being given any moral standards;
lacking in self-discipline? Don't we realise that this is the
root of the problem?'*

All these correspondents (and the thousands they
represent) seem to be saying one basic thing about
our society. When you go secular, casting adrift from
religious moorings, what suffers is persons, personality, personalness. And since the secular process talks
loudly about humanity and human-ness in a 'civilised
society' as its own ideal, something would appear to
be seriously wrong within that process itself. It does
not achieve its own aims.

Christians, of course, have a word for 'not achiev-
ing aims' in that way, and the word is 'sin'. This is
but one illustration of the ways in which an old-
fashioned and generally discarded word can be re-
habilitated within a contemporary context.

One aspect of 'sin', as we have said, is the inability
totally to achieve the target in even our best and
most worthy intentions. We know this personally,
but what the correspondence has thrown into relief
is the way the same 'principle' works in the things we
do corporately. People wrote about the need for and
the rightness of the welfare state in its caring for the

poor and the temporarily needy, yet concerned about those aspects of it which seemed to encourage sloth. Others wrote accepting the fact that we now live in a much more 'open' society, and realising the rightness of that. But a mother spoke for many when she said, '*the freedom my son and daughter assumed when they chose to ignore Mum and Dad's out-dated restraints, honestly hasn't payed them off as they expected. I think sometimes they are pretty near admitting it has turned sour in their mouths*'. Underlying letters like this was the realisation that there is this 'principle' at work in our corporate actions, and that laws which are passed apparently and sincerely intended to defend or increase the individual's freedom and self-determination, may end up somewhere along the line devaluing him, and making real freedom more difficult. Certainly human relationships are the ultimate testing-point where laws and corporate decisions in society are concerned, and a great proportion of the correspondence commented from this angle.

Why not just 'others first' then?

Why not make a determined effort at a less selfish corporate life-style? Someone even proposed adopting one of the Ten Commandments as theme for each year. Clean up adultery this year, move on to stealing next year, then care of the aged! Keep at it, year by year. Put others before self.

From Essex came the suggestion, '*There is a lot to be said for the one good turn a day — it imposes a discipline.*

To the sophisticated this sounds very childish, but one can't read without first mastering the alphabet.'

There was a good deal of power in this particular thrust in the correspondence. It is pretty near the heart of British folk-religion, of course, and people still give it lip-service at least. *'A compassionate regard for the less fortunate and a kindly tolerance to others.'* *'decent standards and a set of values.'* Many who wrote like that were absolutely sincere (*'not a do-gooder'* said one.).

A London correspondent wanted some very practical first steps to be suggested. (*'stopping throwing litter and empty tins onto the road, taking seriously the fraud involved in using expired tickets on the railway, stopping vandalism in trains and buses'*).

Another person who had reached *'the firm conclusion that in the Bible you had all that was needed to guide you to a full and worthwhile life'*, had a go at spelling out what would happen if we took 'Thou shalt not steal' seriously.

'Suppose, suddenly, people stopped stealing and applied this in its widest sense, not only to the actual physical taking of goods. Shoplifting, when I last saw the figure, is running at an incredible £350,000,000 a year. If this be stopped, what an effect this would have on prices — let alone the cost to shops, etc. of massive security arrangements. If people stopped stealing other people's husbands and wives; if people admitted that to take money for a job and not to do it properly was a disguised form of stealing from an employer; if people repaid money promptly and admitted that if you borrow money or obtain credit and then do not repay when expected you are, in effect, living on money that rightly

belongs to someone else. Would not a massive STOP STEALING campaign, backed by the media, work a small miracle in our society if successful?' (Adding a footnote to say that stealing in one form or another marks every section of our society.)

There were those on the other hand who could not believe we would ever behave humanly to our fellows while our society countenanced so many cruelties to animals and to nature. *'As we treat all creation we set in motion good or evil vibrations . . .'* said a correspondent from Sussex, and listed fourteen black spots to tackle first (from vivisection to *'bull fighting kept alive by British tourists'*).

Many more, however, paid tribute to those who *do* care for the elderly, and the disabled, who *do* spend hours with the depressed and the disturbed, who *do* give to those organisations which serve the disadvantaged in our communities.

Others go on struggling, and hoping it is not them who have got it wrong. A university professor, giving his own answers to the question 'What sort of society do I want to live in' included these descriptions:

'A soft-hearted society which loves (but does not spoil, indulge or worship) the young, the old or the minorities, and so makes sure all three are properly cared for.

'A public-spirited society where those who have, give their love, time, energy and money to those who have not, without expecting any honours or material rewards.'

A fascinating comment came from a Nigerian who was visiting England at the time of the 'Call', and felt constrained to write five long pages to the Archbishop. He concluded, *'It is quite simple, really.*

All you have to do is to be kind to your husband, your wife, your children, and above all to your old parents. Share and give happiness and you will receive measure for measure. You cannot lose — it is a law of nature. Go out of your way to be kind as often as the opportunity comes your way. Visit, phone, greet your old parents. They may not understand why you care and may not even thank you, but their hearts will bless you and when you are old too, your children will treat you with equal care and love.'

But through many other letters there ran a fear that maybe we were near the end of the road where all this was concerned. Rather like church-going, it appeared to have the wholehearted support of only a minority, and that minority partly ancient, partly modern, but somehow not including many of the younger middle-age group.

'Having concern for others in this materialistic age is such a rare quality that people are inclined to think there is some ulterior motive in one so motivated as to want to help others.'

'I was trying to get young staff to deal properly with people, and to put the other person first. I got my answer from a twenty-one-year-old: "we look after ourselves, it's self first here".'

A mother wrote about the special problems she faced in her own family, and concluded *'help us all to keep fighting for the survival of a Christian England'*. She echoed many others.

Much of this reflects what has been talked about since at least the end of World War 1 as evidence that a country cannot go on for ever 'living on spiritual capital'. 'Putting others first' is not a natural process, a cultural pattern which can be fostered and maintained merely by wishing it were so. Some, indeed, find it easier than others. Every generation and every culture has its naturally gracious and outward-going individuals, who are an essential ingredient in communities that are not going to come apart at the seams. We seemed to be relying increasingly on such people and families today.

But the Archbishop, in the shorthand of the 'Call' was pointing to the need to sustain and actually increase the number and power of this group when he put the God-framework around them, 'God first, others next, self last'.

A lady in Lancashire was pointing the same moral when she made this rather contentious observation about the architect of the welfare state, '*I learned from the experience of Beveridge that humanism is not enough. His Plan got nowhere because he had no faith in anyone but his fellow men.*'

God first

Most of the Archbishop's correspondents wanted him to fill in the gaps in what he had said. One or two, on the other hand, felt he could have said it all in a text from the Sermon on the Mount.

The favourite was Matthew 6: 33, 'Seek ye *first* the Kingdom of God and His righteousness, and all these things shall be added unto you'. Someone commented: '*This is good economics as well as being religious. O.A.P.s e.g. would not be destitute if we remembered the fourth commandment and did something about it each week.'*

Another was Matthew 6: 19–20, 'Do not store up for yourselves treasure on earth, where it grows rusty and moth-eaten, and thieves break in to steal it (and inflation does so without anybody actually doing anything), but store up treasure in heaven'.

Sayings of Jesus like these, or the Archbishop's words in the 'Call', fall down however, when increasing numbers of those who hear them can give little or no content to the word 'God'.

A lady in Essex wrote to say 'You *know that God comes first of course, but there is no "Of course" for those of us who don't know God. I think you are starting at the wrong end. All of us, you and I, have one thing in common — our interest in our selves — that is universal. Therefore any lead must be centred on that basic interest.'*

Many others wrote in this same way, asking the Archbishop not to take even '*simple, basic religious things for granted*'. For the most part this was not rejection of those religious concepts, rather than a plea for help in bringing them down to understandable everyday contexts.

A Yorkshire correspondent said, '*Your first injunction was to God. That is O.K. provided you* know *that God is. You yourself know* — *but there are tens of thousands who don't, and who say, "Why should we base our behaviour on the discipline of this mythical person?"* '

A lady on the Isle of Wight offered her own interpretation for today of the Ten Commandments. The last six, which concern our neighbourly responsibilities are straightforward: '*Respect those in authority; You shall not kill nor use violence or stealth to injure body, mind, spirit or property; You shall not be rude or incontinent, but master of your passions, and love purely; You shall not steal — nor "pinch" nor "fiddle"; You shall not slander — nor tell lies; You shall not covet — be greedy or jealous, but be content.'*

But with the first four, which centre on our responsibilities to God, she struggled with this same theological, communication problem. Her suggestions were, *'There is only one way — the right way, by conscience; You shall not be obsessed by objects or considerations of material value — not money, jewels, clothes, possessions, pride, drugs, sex; A solemn promise shall be kept; Take time to renew a quiet spirit — and allow it in others.'* This was her attempt to find *'a new avenue to explore, that fits, in the light of new knowledge, while not departing from the true precepts of ancient times'.*

What happened to Jesus?

For every ten who wrote of their difficulties over the religious words he had used, a hundred were worried over those the Archbishop had left out.

First, there were large numbers who looked in vain for an Old Testament style call to national repentance, failing to discern it in his *'too gentle approach'.*

From Essex, *'As a nation we have rejected God and broken all His laws and are now reaping the consequences. In your position, you have a great responsibility to call the nation back to God. If this does not happen, God's judgments are surely coming upon us. Please read Jeremiah 26: 13 ("if you now mend your ways and your doings and obey*

the Lord your God, then he may relent and revoke the dis-
aster with which he has threatened you"), and speak out
boldly for Christ.'

A retired naval officer wanted the same thing, but
feared that 'our country as a whole can only expect to go
through a pretty chaotic period brought on by envy, greed
and covetousness allied with indiscipline. All of us are
guilty in varying degrees and so must expect to suffer a bit
of the old Jehovah treatment which I hope against hope will
not be too severe. (But cannot be the soft approach to
criminal actions and lowered standards that are now the
"in thing".)'

From Birmingham came this view: 'The moral
condition of Britain today is very largely due to the failure
of the Churches to preach that "God now commandeth all
men everywhere to repent" . . . There must be enough
Christians, deeply conscious of their short-comings, earnestly
crying to God concerning themselves and identifying themselves also with the sins of their fellows as did the Old
Testament prophets.'

'The Word of God does promise revival and deliverance
to "all who call on the name of the Lord" (Joel 2: 32).
Who knows but God himself how much time there is left to
turn to him with all our hearts, both nationally and
individually.'

Secondly, there were those who missed the
directly evangelistic challenge. Only a 'national
revival' would achieve anything, so why paddle in
the shallow waters of social economics and public
morals?

A lady wrote from the South Coast: 'The only way
of revival for the nation is to acknowledge our sins to the

Lord, and to seek earnestly by prayer and fasting that he would have mercy upon us.'

A *'very ordinary person'* believed *'the only thing that can save our country is a spiritual revival. A moral revival does not go deep enough.'*

A group of young people wrote: *'What are you doing towards a revival of religion? It is all very well collecting all this money towards the repair of your Cathedral, but what about the* people? *Do try to perform this miracle through Almighty God. Otherwise, what matters if the magnificent Cathedral does crumble to pieces slowly but surely; People are doing this, so why not the Cathedral? See to Christ's people first.'*

From Scotland came this hope: *'I believe that you have opened the door for Biblical Christianity to be brought to the fore — before the nation. We now have a unique opportunity for setting it forth in a way that can meet modern man's needs — knowing that the Lord has said, "My Word shall not return unto me void". Who knows but that it may please him to pour out his Spirit in mercy on this nation, and send a sweeping revival. Without God's altering our hearts, a solution to today's needs will never be found, no matter what any political party may do.'*

So, thirdly, there were those many who asked, *'What happened to Jesus?'* in the Archbishop's 'Call'.

'I am entirely behind you in your efforts to bring our nation back to morality and sanity, but can this be achieved without the help of Jesus Christ?' asked a Dorset correspondent.

An elderly lady was pleased the Archbishop had invited people to write to him, because she wanted to raise the same point, *'Please forgive me if I seem impertinent, I do not mean to be, but as you were reported in* The Times, *you seem not to have spoken the name of Jesus Christ. God, yes. But not Jesus. Also, I could not quite understand what you meant by "a sense of moral purpose". I should have thought that what they needed to rekindle is the absolute certainty that our Lord Jesus Christ is living and moving about among us here and now.'*

A shop-floor worker in Lancashire wrote, '*There being only one way that is true, and that is by Jesus Christ, it is time we as a nation turned to God again.*' And from nearby someone else said, '*the only hope for the nation or individuals is turning to Jesus Christ*'.

'*What the country needs is Jesus Christ and not just a new code of ethics.*'

Many correspondents told the Archbishop their own story of '*repentance and faith*', their discovery of a living experience of Jesus Christ. Many were still joyfully '*up in the clouds*' after a charismatic experience, identifying as fellow-believers, but not really convinced about the need to speak to the nation's practical problems. Thus a university lecturer, '*I know Jesus as a person, and tend therefore to speak less in terms of Christianity, more in terms of Jesus Christ ... Surely we must all not only stand up and declare ourselves to be Christians — expounding all that this implies — but also and above all declare that Jesus Christ is not the perfect answer in terms of social, economic and political situations, but that he is alive — a real person?*'

The Archbishop's 'Watchnight' address on TV on New Year's Eve must have pleased these correspondents, if they were watching, for he was very simply commending his Lord to his viewers. He

began by recalling his Enthronement service when
'I asked you to pray for me, for wisdom and strength
and that "I might never let go of the unseen hand
of the Lord Jesus".' He went on in the course of the
service, to ask 'the fundamental question, the root
question, Are you taking Christ seriously?' and to
testify, 'If I had a dozen lives, I know to whose
service I would give them! There is only one Master
worthy of total dedication, and that is the Lord
Christ . . . for with his companionship and in the
strength of his Spirit, you face the future with an
inner serenity which belongs to the heirs of those to
whom he made his priceless legacy: "Peace is my
parting gift to you." '

Again, preaching in Canterbury some months
after the 'Call', the Archbishop concluded, 'If I
asked you this question: "What do you believe is
Britain's greatest need today?", what would you
reply? A halt to inflation? A recovery of our old
world position? A higher level of prosperity? Let me
tell you how I would answer my own question. I
would do it very simply. I would say: "Britain's
greatest need today is an army — an army of men
and women, young and old, who line up with Simon
Peter and say, out of a deep conviction: Lord, to
whom can we go? You have the words of eternal
life. We are your men, your women, and we will
follow you to the death. No scoffing for us. No
procrastination. We believe that you are God's
answer to our need, as a race, as a nation, as individuals. In your infinite mercy, you came to meet
us. In our infinite need we look to you."

'That way lies the answer to our need. That way lies hope. That way lies eternal life.'

Are there two Archbishops of Canterbury then? Has he changed his mind and his approach as he went along? Dr. Coggan answers these questions himself in an address which he gave to the British Association in 1967, and which draws the two approaches together.

'There are forces at work which make for hate and wrong and ugliness, forces of great power and mighty malevolence. World forces are engaged. Every human being is, willy-nilly, in the battle. If one thinks to opt out, one finds oneself on the side of evil, for "he that is not with me is against me". But if a man dares to pray with any fullness of meaning the prayer "Thy kingdom come", he lines himself up with the forces of right and does his tiny part in making the reign of God a reality in the world of space and time.

'But *how* is the Kingdom to come and who are to be the agents of its coming? There have been those down the ages — and there are still some today — who answer simply: "The agents of the Kingdom are the members of the Church of Christ". I believe they are right and they are wrong — right in their emphasis; wrong in their implied exclusiveness.

'I believe that he alone can *fully* pray this prayer who consciously and of his own free will lives his life, does his work, thinks out his philosophy, in obedience to Jesus Christ. But to put the statement "the agents of the Kingdom are the members of the Church of Christ" thus baldly, is to refuse to face facts and to be guilty of an inadequate doctrine of God the Holy Spirit. Wherever truth — in the realms of theology or philosophy, of the arts or of the sciences — invades the territory of darkness, ignorance and error, there the Spirit of Truth is at work. Wherever the forces of disease and death are conquered, there the Spirit of Life is operating. Wherever ugliness is kept at bay, there the Spirit of God who is the God of Beauty is doing his creative and re-creative labour.'

The Archbishop's reply to those who ask 'What happened to Jesus?' therefore can be summed up in another question, 'What do you think the Father and the Spirit are doing in our world?'

'God is not some kind of super-ecclesiastic interested only in Churchly things, as many imagine him to be, but the God behind all discovery and invention and learning, the Source of all truth, the Origin of all beauty. And *therefore* — and this is the point to which I am leading up — whoever he be who is an agent of that work, in laboratory or study of studio or slum, is a servant of the Most High, an agent of the King, even though he be not conscious of that fact in all its glory (and therefore, I think, immeasurably the poorer!).'

Why don't you call us to prayer?

In his post after the 'Call' the Archbishop faced an avalanche of requests to consider another possible line of action which would affect, people believed, the whole life of the nation.

'May I humbly request you to call another National Day of Prayer such as we had in the war?' (There were hundreds and hundreds, who made the same request.)

'Why not ask the BBC to reintroduce Big Ben at nine o'clock so that there could be a daily minute of recollection by as many as could use it that way?' (and many correspondents sent in booklets from World War II testifying to how this had been done by thousands then).

'I sit most mornings with my coffee and listen to, and join in the Service on Radio 4. In this short time if all the people who are at home could just spend those fifteen minutes united in prayer and thought, I'm sure God would work through that medium for good.'

These three specific suggestions are different from each other in kind. The last is one which is no doubt already largely fulfilled by many of those who can regularly listen to the BBC Daily Service. The second, were there to be sufficient public pressure, is no doubt one the BBC would consider, since the Nine O'clock News has to be introduced in one way or another, and Big Ben is associated with it by tradition. The use certain people in the country chose to make of that minute would not be something for which the BBC or anyone else would be in any way responsible. (Indeed there would appear to be no reason why those who wished should not use the nine o'clock moment for prayer for the nation whatever the current format for introducing the TV News!)

But a National Day of Prayer is another matter

altogether. On this question the Archbishops have had to declare their minds. In the decades since World War II (as the correspondence has borne constant record as we have gone along), the general tone of British Society has become less and less traditionally 'Christian'. Whether we check this against church-going statistics, baptism and confirmation figures, marriage and divorce trends, or the sort of factors we have been examining before, the facts seem to be established. A 'Call to Prayer' today therefore, would not be the same as thirty years ago. It would very likely be heeded by, at the most, the numbers of those who are in churches at Christmas or Easter (perhaps ten per cent of the nation). In these circumstances, there is likely to be greater benefit in the churches pursuing their regular efforts at involving more people in their weekly offering of prayer to God.

Even more important would be the implication in having a *Day* of Prayer, that somehow God is a God of the emergency situation, and that you can change his mind by a one-off approach. This does not tally with the Bible's teaching on, or Christ's practice of, prayer as a regular, sustained effort. Yet one has to record a certain wonder at the sheer volume of pressure for such a Day in the Archbishop's letters.

What also emerged many times in the correspondence was how inadequately church people felt themselves trained for praying, whether for the nation, or indeed, generally. Yet it is here that the strength to 'put the other fellow first' is to be found. Some of the groups which have begun in answer to the 'Call' have tried to include praying in their activity, so that it might spread back into family and everyday life.

The Nigerian correspondent I quoted earlier, had something to say about this too, '*I pray that you, my brothers and sisters, black and white, in Europe, should form the* habit *of regular prayer in your family unit, i.e., share your problems and praises with each other and with God. I also pray that you will soon regain your faith and understanding of God.*'

A family near London who wrote about a simpler life-style suitable for today, linked it with praying like this: '*We are well aware of the terrible lack of everything in the Third World. We suggest having a day of starvation to be spent in silence, prayer and reading. The money we save on such a day could be sent to buy a meal for one poor family.*' Another strong link between praying and 'others'.

Self last?

There is one last strand of correspondence to be considered before we leave this. Most people who wrote about 'God first, others next, self last' accepted its shorthand headline style. A church organist who had never preached a sermon in his life (but sounded as if he would have liked to have been asked), wrote, '*In all the years I have been listening to two sermons per Sunday, I do not remember hearing* even *one on some words which came from our Lord himself, and which stated clearly what each individual must do to follow him* . . .

"*If any man would come after me, let him deny himself, take up his cross daily, and follow me*" (*Luke 9: 23*). *As I understand it, I hope correctly, the cross we are told to take up daily is the abnegation of self in the loving service of our fellow-men.*'

But another correspondent (one of a number who were too shy to put their address on their letters) made this shrewd comment: ' "*God — others — self*": *this is good and helpful to bear in mind, in politics as well as personal matters. But isn't it also open to be misinterpreted, if "self" is thought of, not as the third in importance, but of* no *importance? Of course "self-fulfilment" can be abused, but unless there is respect for the self's possibilities, in what way do we differ from those whose highest value is the state? Surely anyone must feel that his self is his identity, without which he is of no use to others or to God — that self does not only mean self-indulgence, that the pleasure we get from serving is a part of ourselves.*'

A number of others drew attention to this. '*The need for self-affirmation before one can effectively be much use to others is implicit in Christ's command to "love your neighbour as yourself". The whole modern psychological approach, properly understood, (as in Jack Dominian's "Cycles of Affirmation", e.g.), underlines this basic understanding. This sees Christ himself as the Man who fully accepted, affirmed and loved his own being because his Father first loved him. A stress on self-denial when it is not preceded by having come to terms with the 'I' which is myself, can lead to un-Christ-like behaviour in fact.*'

But this is to go deeper, and at another angle than was intended in the Archbishop's words.

Questions

1. Have another look at Question 4 on p. 46. Would you want to alter your answer to it in the light of having thought further now about the effects of secular society on the 'personal-ness' of life?

2. Is there adequate reason to let 'the other fellow matter' if you have no special religious motive for doing so?

3. Where would you look for help in trying to pray effectively?

4. Do you believe that God would today give us '*a bit of the old Jehovah treatment*'? What does this expression conjure up in your mind? Does God work like that or through the inevitable processes we bring upon ourselves?

5. Why do you think the Church today is not more successful in her direct evangelism? How could she do better locally where you live?

6. Self-indulgence (bad) is not the same as 'accepting' and living with ourselves as we are (good). Can you work out another formula like 'God first — others next — self last' which would get round the objections that were raised?

6

Attitudes Matter

THIS FINAL STATEMENT by the Archbishop had to do with materialism, and sparked off a further bout of deeply radical questioning among his correspondents.

What he actually said was:

'Of course we need money. We must think about money, but if we think of nothing else except money — and we are getting dangerously near that sorry state today — the standards of our life will decline, yes, even in the material sphere! Stark materialism does not work. It does not deliver the goods. We must adopt a different attitude to money, and to materials, and to machines. They are useful servants, but they are degrading masters. It is the kind of people who handle them that matters, and what their attitudes to life are. So stop making money the priority.'

This was traditional enough — yet sounded crudely abrasive to many who had either never questioned the style of our society, or had come to the conclusion you could do nothing but harm in raising such questions.

A Sussex correspondent said it all '*sounds to me strangely unreal when we live in a society that is based on materialism. By asking people to "stop making money the priority", are you not seeking a break-down of your whole way of life? Or is it that you only expect some people to follow this advice? A little personal piety amid a great ideal of greed and self-seeking?*'

'*A certain West country M.P. in his maiden speech in 1970 said that the kind of society he was striving for was one in which any man could by his own efforts become a millionaire. This does to me sum up, albeit rather crudely, what our society is about. Do you really mean "stop making money the priority"? The consequences of this would be catastrophic. Or do you mean "temper your search for wealth and material prosperity with a little moderation"?*'

A lady in the South brought up the same theme of the basic motivations of capitalism, '*From our earliest days we are besought to "get on in the world", to get bigger and better positions. On all sides the media of television and advertising tempt and provoke us all to buy and spend — better houses, better cars, colour television — the list is endless and only leads to more "getting and spending".*'

A London housewife added, '*To take one point, our shops give choices of food which make the mind boggle, and make shopping confusing and more time-consuming. So many varieties, and so many different products of one type of food. Then, the invitations to do everything the quick and easy way, and ultimately the more expensive! TV brainwashing and the encouragement to indulge and spoil oneself . . .*'

And from Yorkshire a retired teacher and Methodist local preacher wrote, '*When children see their parents filling up their "pools" forms every week they begin to believe that what matters in life is not hard work, but "luck".*'

Through all this one is aware of what for many has become the overbearing power of money. But where do you go from there? The Archbishop's words concentrated on the personal response. Here perhaps more than anywhere else in his statements, we see why the Bishop of Southwark said what he said.

He was not alone. A correspondent in Kent wrote: '*You point, quite rightly I think, to increasing selfishness, accompanied by too great a concern for money and material goods and a neglect of spiritual and human values. You imply that this applies, in the main, to the "ordinary" man and that until he changes his attitudes there can be no change for the better generally.*

'*But have you considered that there may be a reason why the moral standards of the "ordinary" man have declined . . . that the basic form of our present society is an immoral one? Its very foundation is ruthlessly material; the economic and therefore political system depends on the search for personal gain. The term "freedom" used so often in our society generally means the freedom to exploit to personal advantage or to act irresponsibly. Leaders and owners set by their example purely material standards, glorifying the wealth and status of privileged individuals (e.g. £205,000 redundancy payments for a top official but £2000 average for the "ordinary" man).*

'*I would suggest to you that it is unreasonable and futile*

*to expect the "ordinary" man to change his attitude until
the basic form of our society is changed. The problems you
describe are largely a condition of the nature of the society
in which we live. Nothing of real value can be achieved
until the form is changed from being a* privately *owned to
a* cooperatively *and responsibly owned society. In short, a
man cannot possibly live a moral life in a society in which
the basic tenets are themselves immoral.'*

The history on our backs

There were four areas in which the sheer weight of
history on our backs made for difficult discussion.

1. THE DEPRESSION

Many correspondents, even those deeply concerned that he should succeed, were suspicious of the
Archbishop's words. We are still too near the 1920s
and 1930s when, so the widely-held story goes, the
Churches did not speak out on behalf of the unemployed and their families. So today any general
statement is likely to be heard as an attack on the
hard-won and still inadequate standards of those
who were children in those sad times.

A correspondent wrote, for example: '*Very often
my work takes me through the Rhondda Valley where, for
all to see, lies the end of the Christian religion in South
Wales. You've left it a bit late to appeal to the people. Too
many are disillusioned. I respect you for I recognise in you
a wise and kindly person of great learning. The tragedy is*

. . . you protect, represent and perpetuate a system isolated from the people. It's members of your class who called, and are still calling, the miners, "enemies of the state". I hope your campaign succeeds, but many of them now are unemployed, and certainly cannot afford to keep a string of horses to play with. You are asking victims to accept more victimisation.'

From the South-West a nurse wrote: *'Whereas people with money have had material things for years, that's O.K., but now because ordinary people are getting more and more material things, that's wrong.'* She, too, like others we have quoted, had *'come to the conclusion that it is the fault of our capitalistic society . . . I was always a staunch conservative but through experience I have decided socialism is fairer to everyone. I have worked in very poor districts. The minute a new-born babe arrives in those houses it is a second-class citizen. That child will grow up spiritually and culturally if not physically deprived.'*

There was plenty of evidence of this close link in people's minds between the Churches, the 'bosses' and the assumptions of capitalistic society (whether it be, as the Archbishop of York has recently been reminding his viewers on TV, private or state capitalism).

A London worker put it like this: *'Come to think of it, I can't remember hearing any Church leader making a speech on television when the "ugly face of capitalism" was being allowed free reign, when the property speculators were never having it so good, when the working man's organisations were under attack from the government's class legislation . . .'*

And even those who are predisposed to accept what the Archbishop said, or the theme of the Bishop of Winchester's book, *Enough is Enough* (S.C.M. Press), react defensively when it occurs to them that simplifications of our life-style may put people out of work. The shadow of the Depression still broods over any discussion on living standards.

2. PRELACY

'*You live in the comfort of a Palace. You have a guaranteed income. Your appeal to the nation rings rather hollow.*' Those three sentences from a letter from Cambridgeshire summarise one correspondent's views, and incidentally reflect the substance of many hundreds of others.

'*You yourself live in a Palace with many assistants and all modern comforts including a wage about four times as much as the average man earns. Jesus Christ also scorned the pursuit of material gain but at least he practised what he preached. Until the Establishment starts ruling by example I'm afraid many people will not be prepared to take you seriously.*'

A member of what he called '*a classless Pentecostal Church*' in the Home Counties, was even more insistent. '*The reason the C. of E. churches are being emptied is because of people like you who associate with the earls, lords, kings and ruling classes and then call upon ordinary people to make sacrifices! Call for sacrifice at the top end first, and, on seeing it, you'll get some response from the average man-in-the-street.*'

A sign of Establishment attacked by some of the

Archbishop's correspondents was the presence in the House of Lords of some senior bishops. From the industrial North came the cry, '*I would like to suggest that the Church could commence a vast purging of the social and economic impurities endemic in this rotten state of capitalism, by rejecting out of hand and forthwith your and your bishops' seats in the House of Lords.*'

This sort of reaction is somehow implicit in the discussion when an archbishop (or a cabinet minister or an industrialist or a merchant banker, or, increasingly these days, a top and powerful T.U. figure) raises such issues. '*He's all right*'. '*He's not one of us*'. These ordinary human beings with top jobs to do must be (despite all we know of them) '*greedy graspers after the spoils of office, ruthless protectors of their status and riches*'. This applies, apparently, even in those cases where we know this to be palpable nonsense.

We have reached the stage, maybe, where even a gesture like that of the Archbishop and some other bishops in rejecting salary increases, becomes self-defeating. Someone wrote about this, '*Frankly I think it is silly. It panders to the materialistic streak in us, and does not help the nation one little bit. It panders to, rather than helps cope with, envy.*' And from Hampshire, in a certain cynical despair, a lady said, '*I cannot but agree with those who are saying "What is the point of making the sacrifice when there are such glaring examples of waste and misuse of money being daily reported"?*'

To be fair one has to record, however, that by far the larger number of those who mentioned this, approved of the Archbishop's action as lending credibility to his words.

3. INVESTMENTS

The third bit of history sitting heavily on his back was the invested capital of the Church. Indeed the whole imagery of prelacy, at which we have just looked, is clothed upon and embodied by it. Even if Dr. Coggan and the bishops were to go barefoot and threadbare around the land, having renounced their share in the use of the Church's inherited wealth, the argument would still remain. '*How can a Church that pretends to serve Jesus Christ, live largely on its invested funds, and play the capitalist market in order to get richer?*'

A worker in the North wrote, '*You speak of greed for money, and pour scorn on materialism but the Church is one of the biggest upholders of this vile and soul-destroying creed.*' He went on to refer to the Church's sale of bombed church sites in city-centres, its investment in the steel (i.e. armaments) industry, and '*its most ungodly stock exchange dealings*'.

And from Berkshire an angry letter spoke of the unavailability even of Church buildings for community use very often. '*How can you justify buildings which stand idle all week whilst I run a voluntary service for decorating for elderly and handicapped people and can't get any storage space? Or where I used to live, the Cathedral aloof with its chamber music and intellectuals living in their escapism world?*'

Yet, as so often there was another side to all this.

A country vicar with no shade of complaining or comparison implied, just asked the Archbishop to remember that not all people were even in the position to be tempted by materialism. *'I am un-ashamedly concerned about money. I am concerned that I haven't enough to do my job properly. I am concerned because my parishioners, some of them at least, are going without the things that I ought to be able to provide and be glad to give them, i.e., a visit in emergencies, just because there is no petrol in the tank, and no money in the pocket to buy more; or that there is petrol only sufficient to provide transport for my wife to go to work.'*

4. INDIVIDUALISM

Whether in the Coggan-Stockwood incident, or more generally in the whole correspondence, it is obvious that a fourth weight on our backs is the centuries-old heresy of Western man in over-emphasising the aspects of life he calls 'individual', as against the corporate aspects which all too quickly he labels and rejects, or labels and hides behind. A Scot wrote sympathetically but with concern at this, *'I read with interest of your "Call". What you suggest is quite right, and even, if universally accepted, revolutionary. However, as a Christian, it grieves me that whenever the voice of the Church is heard, no serious criticism of "structural" evil seems to come across. The demonic surely expresses itself in man's inhumanity to man, and our attack on this ought not to be concentrated on the individual level (pull up your spiritual socks) to the exclusion of the level at which men affect one another via major and*

*apparently amoral structures. I support you, but pray that
we might not be forced to be puppets of the vested interest
which we all have in the Western world.'*

People wrote to the Archbishop with ideas about
this. Another Scot, perhaps with business interests in
Japan, saw the particular factory or firm as the right
corporate unit to work on. *'Pick a day — a weekday —
to have a service first, then free all day. A communal service
— wives and all — generates splendid spirit. Go further,*
and pick a patron saint!'

The same correspondent would like to see bishops
in industrial dioceses as members of the Institute of
Directors, spending time impressing on their fellow
directors the need to take the initiative, by example
and by word, in bringing goodwill and better morale
into their companies. *'It cannot always be the wicked
shop-steward who is to blame. The move has got to come
from the top.'*

Both these ideas, of course, involve working within
the given system, not attempting to replace it by
another. Throughout these letters however, has come
the question whether we ought to go on assuming
that small reforms are enough, or whether we ought
not rather to face the implications others are making,
that the system itself has to change radically. Behind
the Archbishop of York's comment quoted earlier
('private or state capitalism') is the reminder that
we may only discover as we go along that the
temptations implicit in one system are not necessarily
going to be missing from another.

'Christianity the most materialistic of religions'

Inevitably in an age in which TV has taught us to look for quick controversy, correspondents began remembering Archbishop William Temple's famous saying, and placing it in opposition to Dr. Coggan's words.

A wife in London asked, '*I am curious to know why you are so antagonistic towards "materialism". Materialism, combined with consideration for others, is not a bad thing. It is a quite natural part of man's desire for improvement.*'

Others took up this affirmatory attitude towards life as God has given it to be lived. Someone quoted David Manzie in the Christian newsheet *Challenge*, going back to the Old Testament in its down-to-earth attitude:

'*When the Jews sorted out their money they recognised God as head of state and gave him the first payment. Having paid their dues, they made their other contributions such as looking after families, widows and orphans, and public building. Altogether over one-third of their income went in this way, and after that they gave voluntarily.*

'*So why don't we ask, "what can I put into it?" or "How can I help Britain?" I seem to remember an "I'm backing Britain" campaign, started by five typists in 1968, fizzled out for lack of support. One failure is not final — why not try again?*'

We come back here to the controversy we looked at earlier about 'love of self'. Because too easily the Western emphasis on the individual has led Christians to reject the 'sinful self' and to derive a dynamic from self-hatred and suspicion, we find it hard to *affirm* self today. Yet as Dr. Jack Dominian has said recently, the Christian should be seeking for '*the virtue of reality which, with the minimum of psychological defences, seeks to deny not one iota of our worth, but neither to add one hairbreadth of anything that does not exist. The ultimate goal of love of self is the growth of our potential, for the richer we are, the more we possess ourselves, the more we can give to others and allow us to receive from them.*'

Translating this into the sphere of work, we do well to heed these comments from another correspondent, '*I believe that a source of deep malaise within our society is that we are not able to give thanks to God for the activity by which we live. Despite all the work of industrial mission, we have made no real breakthrough, and there is a widespread feeling in our society that industry and commerce, which are the activities by which this country earns its living, are in some way evil or at best questionable.*' (This goes much deeper than the question of how we organise our production processes, of course.)

'*How different this is when one reflects on farming*', this correspondent went on, and at once brought into play all the British 'villager' fantasies which are so very strong a motivation in advertising. Nevertheless, his point is well made. He concluded, '*One of the marks of the society which we want, in response to your first great question, will be that it will be a society which assumes, affirms and celebrates the value and worthwhileness of the activity by which it lives, while remaining critical of the way in which that activity is organised and performed.*' Here indeed are words that seem to go to the heart of our dilemma. And deeply Biblical words too, for they are affirmative and materialistic in the sense in which Temple used the word.

Materialism is out

Dr. Coggan was clearly using the word differently. He was speaking of 'excess', about which the Bishop of Winchester was writing in *Enough is Enough*. It is the area of greed, of covetousness and envy. In *that* sense materialism cannot 'deliver the goods'. It is a self-defeating tension. Arguably it is an essential dynamic for our sort of society. Those who call it immoral, do so for this reason. 'More' is never enjoyed for its own sake before being overtaken by the next wave of inner restlessness and impatience for still more. This is a dehumanising, sterile process. Keeping up with the Joneses is almost always at the expense of the people next door the other way. In terms the world understands, the Archbishop was telling the dismal truth.

Provided *that* materialism is out, then we know what Temple meant. An artist wrote from Scotland, quoting Père Tielhard, '*It is in intelligent alliance with the rising tides of matter that we shall draw nearer to the Spirit.*' She continued, '*I believe that if we handle materialism rightly we shall be nearer to God . . . by giving, not taking. When I have nothing I have everything. The value of the individual is the fact of the One Humanity.*'

Put more simply by two housewives in the South, '*The gigantic task is to prove to the nation, to the world, that there are better things in life than material gains.*'

'*Men think they need so many material things in order to be happy, but it is in finding Christ that this really comes about.*'

If example is more telling than precept, then this letter from Wales is worth quoting. '*For a long time I have worked in business mostly in London and I have become increasingly conscious of the shallow and spiritually unrewarding consequences of such a life. Some years ago we bought this farm where we have our home and I have been progressively transferring my activities and shortly I hope to be here full time. I mention this because I feel I am one of the fortunate who have had the opportunity to discover the happiness and fulfilment which comes from pursuing a life which is not principally motivated by making money and acquiring material possessions. I firmly believe that many people in this country feel this way and will be helped by what you are trying to do.*'

And this advertisement in a trade journal: '*We offer you our nine point fair trading deal — Honest straightforward dealing: Integrity: Sincerity: Non-misrepresentation of goods availability; Square deal: Fair play: Service backed by goods: Technical ability above average: A genuine desire on our part to further the case of (the hobby we exist to serve), to the benefit of all concerned.*'

The proprietors went on: '*We believe that today, more than at any other time in our history, Great Britain needs men of courage and honesty, with goodwill and the ability to withstand the despicable standards so rife in our present society which threatens to destroy us. We are trying to do our part to put our country back on the map. Are you? Support the men of goodwill.*'

Great Britain?

Two mentions of our country in that way in this chapter raise the question, finally; is this call to patriotism one which means much any longer? Or is it all so sullied with the less acceptable memories of our history (some of which we have briefly looked at above) that it can no longer be credibly used?

Should it be used anyhow? asked a London lady. '*Are you not encouraging a narrow nationalism? We are told to seek the Kingdom of God, not the sort of country we want England to be. Caesar only has the superscription.*'

Numbers of those who received the Prayer Card took the trouble to write back making this same point. One wrote from North London, '*Thank you for sending me the Prayer Card. I should like to make some comments on this.* '*On the back you write* . . . "*There are a great many who are deeply concerned about* '*the economy of our nation*'."'

'*Why are most of us* "*deeply concerned*"*? Because it is going to make a difference to our life-style — because automatic rises in pay will have to stop — because prices are going up. But we should be concerned, not only about the economy of our nation, but because of the fact that our nation, and all the other rich nations are all the time getting richer, while the poor nations are getting poorer — and why? Because the rich nations are exploiting the poor nations, and have been doing so for years and the situation is getting worse all the time.*

'*Serious-minded people should have been* "*deeply con-cerned*" *very many years ago — and it has come to this — all the money in so-called "Aid" — and investment that we send to the developing world is exceeded by the money they have to send to us — so, we are getting richer at their expense — and why do we have to tolerate having to be part of a community in which everything we pay — taxes etc. is helping to starve more babies and kill more people among our brothers in the poor world?*

'*But your call to prayer is about the economy of our nation. This means that I cannot use this prayer — I am more a citizen of the world than of any nation and have always thought that Jesus meant that to follow him would be a call to brotherhood of all men.*'

A clergyman working for a development agency wrote: '*You speak of the need for a "better Britain", but there would be many of us who would say that we do have a "better Britain" now than, say, between the wars, in many important aspects.*

'*In terms of the "developing world" we are rightly concerned to try to identify the inarticulate and completely impoverished people of these countries, so that we can help them. We are rightly concerned that a large part of the wealth of the developing countries is in the hands of a relatively few people, and feel it should be spread for the benefit of the whole people of the country. Surely this same argument should also in fairness apply to our own country? I could not accept that those of us who wish to see a fairer distribution are motivated by envy alone: rather we see it as a matter of justice.*'

Many correspondents linked Great Britain, her rôle in the world now, and this sense of responsibility for others in the global family, with present levels of expenditure on defence. Even after all the recently announced 'cuts' have taken effect, said one family, '*a huge proportion of the nation's wealth is devoted to the build-up of armaments which can never afford genuine security, and which only increased the fears which are one of the main causes of war*'. They continued on the matter of positive peace-making, pointing towards another possible rôle for Britain. '*At present the only people that can be sent to areas of tension are those trained in military methods inappropriate to peace-making. There is need for a body of people trained on more positive lines, including the practice of non-violence, which is coming to be recognised as the best answer to violence and aggression.*' Finally they pleaded that overseas aid levels should be raised, saying that '*some of the funds required could well come from money saved on armaments*'.

World peace, expenditure on armaments, Britain's rôle in international peace-keeping, came up again and again. Among a significant section of those who wrote to the Archbishop, the whole threat of war and the nation's responsibility in international affairs was top priority.

Where Dr. Coggan stands on these issues he put succinctly in the little S.P.C.K. booklet on 'The Christian Faith':

'Man is involved in a corporate wrongness for which he is not as an individual wholly responsible. "All have sinned". There is an infection of human nature which breaks out from time to time in corporate acts of awfulness such as war. The Christian, as a member of the "new creation" of those who have availed themselves of Christ's redemption, must declare himself utterly opposed to force as a means of settling quarrels (even though he realises that Christians are divided among themselves on the issue of pacifism). He stands behind such a statement as Resolution 106 of the Lambeth Conference 1958: "The Conference affirms that war as a method of settling international disputes is incompatible with the teaching and example of our Lord Jesus Christ and declares that nothing less than the abolition of war itself should be the goal of the nations, their leaders, and all citizens." '

The implications of all this, in these letters, was that true patriotism could not be seen as a narrowly self-centred matter. It was rather that development of good neighbourliness and responsibility as a nation, wanting to be our best for the sake of greater world happiness and justice and peace. This came through the letters about disarmament, and about world development, and about missionary responsibility. It had obvious links with the main themes of the Old Testament. God's people were to be a working model of his 'Kingdom', not so that they themselves would be more materially prosperous (though this might well happen). Rather, their own success was to be seen openly in the light of their having put God first and others next. They were called as 'light to lighten the Gentiles' (privileged *for the sake of the underprivileged*, developed *for the sake of the underdeveloped*).

By and large they failed to fulfil that calling.

Questions

1. How far do you feel the Church is still justifiably branded as Establishment, part of the capitalistic machinery of state?

2. Is there any way in which to answer the needs of the clergyman on p. 135 and many like him, except by going on investing the Church's capital profitability?

3. If the Archbishops had sounded a Call which had been about the structures of our society, what should it have said? And how do you imagine it would have been heard?

4. Materialism, 'yes' and 'no'. Consider these sections of this chapter (pp. 137–140) by taking the specific question 'For how much is it right to insure my life, and on what grounds do I make a "right" decision?'

5. Why are most people bored by the development aid discussion now? How can we overcome 'compassion fatigue' in the TV age?

7

What Sort of Society?
What Sort of People?

27,000 was no sort of a scientific sampling of public opinion. Those who wrote decided for themselves. There was no control of the response. It is impossible therefore to use this self-selected group, and their views, as some sort of poll of what 'people' feel today.

On the other hand, many of these letters were quite obviously first-timers. *'I have never written to an Archbishop before'* must often have meant *'I have never written this sort of letter before.'* There was high motivation involved. And presumably for every letter that was written, several others only just missed being written. This was some sort of an indication of what many people felt strongly enough about to put into a letter.

They had a fairly provocative occasion for doing so. The Archbishop had not exactly minced his words. Even so, with these provisos, I think we are justified in making some tentative comments on the state of things in our nation today as the letters reveal it.

In the process of drawing this book together, I have had the benefit of comparing my own assessment of what people felt to be important with the statements of many of the new groups which have begun discussing these questions. Such statements have begun to be sent to the Archbishop recently, a second wave of the 'Call' correspondence. In it all it becomes apparent that we *know* we are at a cross-roads.

Future Shock is written all over it, that is to say, everyone is aware, increasingly aware, of major changes in our social patterns, and the still greater changes these seem to make necessary.

We have, for instance, looked briefly at four areas of our common life which are in process of very rapid change, and which call for radical long-term reassessment at once.

First, *our economic and monetary system*, in the world context from which it can never pretend to stand aloof. It is not only industrial or banking 'colds' in America or Geneva that give us pneumonia now. We do not only have 'a moral responsibility' to do something fairer about the Third World: primary producers have power to cause us to do so. David Edward's *The State of the Nation* (Church Information Office) spells it all out.

Secondly, *our political system*, with its efforts to cope with the changing focus of power in society. Parliament — Cabinet — T.U.C. — C.B.I., maybe one or two of the main unions as an almost separate power entity of their own — E.E.C. — the bankers.

A London consultant spoke for many when he wrote, '*What I resent is the tendency to divide us all into factions: working class vs. managers; public schools vs. comprehensives; council house occupier vs. home-owner — to oppose each other and destroy us all. Unfortunately, politics makes the divisions even deeper.'*

Another Londoner said, *'We, the public, know something you do not know: as things are in our society, men and women count for less each year. Our vote under the present system counts for less and less; our voice hardly ever reaches the seat of power which isolates itself more effectively from us year by year. We feel increasingly more unimportant. The "system" has become greater than human beings. This is why we are cynical. We know that cynicism is better than revolution. We also know that these are the only two alternatives. Because the controllers of the "system" (be it government, commerce or industry or — yes, even the church) plough relentlessly on, ignoring your statement that people count.*

'This is how it feels to us. A denial of our feelings does not alter them. A recognition of our feelings might. I would have warmed to you if you had said: "I know that you feel that your voice and your vote count for nothing. I know it, because I have felt the same way myself quite frequently. I shall probably find out all over again as a result of this appeal of mine. But never mind, let us find out how we can together change the situation, so that your voice and vote count for something." '

Thirdly, *our education system.* Whilst we go on adapting our present systems and trying to get the statistics right for a good teacher-pupil ratio, for a fairer distribution of resources so that the underprivileged can catch up a bit, and for a better spread of educational opportunities over the age ranges, tomorrow's questions stare us in the face. What forms of education will best fit a normal life-expectancy in which work will no longer dominate to the extent it has done till now? How can 'education for leisure' register with all sorts of people, and cease to be one of the areas in which the 'have's' take up what opportunities exist because very often those opportunities are conceived against a particular educational background? How can education prepare the next-coming generations to cope with the pressures we have been looking at throughout this book?

Fourthly, *our work and rewards system*, still based on a rapidly disappearing set of realities. How long a working week can we allow each other if all are to have the essential human spur of being part of the production processes whereby we survive as a people? How can we discover that affirmation of manufactory and industrial production for which one correspondent rightly pleaded (p. 138)? How can a strong decision to work over a period on reducing overall differentials in reward be taken, so that we can feel we belong to a fair society? What share in reward is rightly measured in job-satisfaction rather than money?

Those are not the only four areas people wrote about, as we have seen. But they seem enough, and important enough, to make my point.

It's all too big for me

People feel all this to be too vast, too threatening. Some, and one can only feel sympathetic towards them, want to bury their heads in the sand.

'*As a great-grandmother of two girls, grandmother of six girls and six boys, and mother of two sons and one daughter, I have feared for the future of them all.*

'*Nowadays, the silent majority is subject to a sense of hopeless pessimism that we of this nation, and of this world, are hell-bent on destruction akin to that of the Gadarene swine — and that it is already too late to avert it.*'

A few, but only a few, wrote asking what all the fuss was about anyhow. A vicar contributing his weekly piece to the local paper at the time of the 'Call' could write, '*You must forgive me if I seem a bit dense this week (more dense than usual, that is) but I find myself rather puzzled as a result of the Archbishop of Canterbury's pep-talk to the nation. Behind his remarks was one clear assumption: we are in a state of crisis.*

'*Dense and obtuse I may well appear but I can't for the life of me work that one out. All right, a number of things in the picture aren't too rosy: prices and costs and the size of the electricity bills, to mention a few. It's true, too, that every time one switches on a news bulletin there's guaranteed to be some dire warning from a haggard-looking government minister. But, without wishing to be unpatriotic or complacent, these are Harold's problems and my heart doesn't really bleed for him. He's got out of more tight corners than most of us have had hot dinners and he'll get out of this one.*'

The same writer went on, '*The only real "crisis" that exists in this country concerns the changing social order of things*', by which he meant the assumption of power by representatives of the workers.

And to the Archbishop, '*I believe you are a humble, very ordinary man, Archbishop, whose greatest gifts to us and the nation are precisely those of humility and ordinary, plain man's sense (at least that's the way you come across to us in your broadcasts). You've reassured some of us that you only live in a flat of your Palace and you've gracefully declined a rise in your salary.*

'*But now, literally for God's sake, don't let them lock you up in your Establishment setting. And please don't join the powerful forces muttering on about crises, just go on showing us how the powerless and those who have still to arrive can be freed and helped on their way.*'

'*A pep-talk about the greed and selfishness of those who have made it and hold the power-strings — now, that would be something. Quite apart from being a little more in line with the Master's sentiments on these matters.*'

Those whose make-up was less placid, perhaps, wanted *action*. No one actually said, '*Stop the world, I want to get off*', but if half the '*bans*' and '*edicts*' and '*warnings*' had been issued that his correspondents urged Dr. Coggan to make, it might have reduced us to half-speed. (Always assuming, of course, that he had been heard!)

Politically, there were many who were looking for a leader figure to emerge from the wings, and to take over. '*Perhaps the need of the hour will bring forward someone of vision and leadership to shock us from our lethargy.*' '*We need a leader, someone to guide us back to sanity and common sense.*'

'*We lack inspired leadership. Political double-talk does not suffice. Most ordinary folk are tired and bored by the present generation of politicians.*' '*Britain's sickness is due to lack of any but the most perfunctory leadership.*'

Sensing, I suppose, that the direction of all this

could be highly dangerous (as someone put it, '*The climate is right for any crank or madman of the extreme right or the extreme left to take over*'), numbers suggested some sort of coalition leadership.

'*A non-party rally of the British people to channel the efforts of all who wish to put our country back on the road to sanity.*'

'*Political leadership which lies in the centre of the two main parties at the moment, and could rise above party politics.*'

Where it all happens

As we have seen, all this scene, threatening to many who have not yet been able to acclimatise, (and are fairly certain they do not want to) bears heaviest upon the individual. For all practical purposes, this still means that the family takes the brunt of whatever strains are around. The evidence drawn upon for this report suggests that the time is ripe for a sober look at the family, if it is indeed the basic institution of the society we want. We are at present imposing upon it all the strains we can, and it is suffering. Few of the attacks are head-on (though many would want to qualify even that statement). Most are incidental to other changes that we can do little about. What would be disastrous would be so to concentrate on relieving other pressures piece-meal, that we failed to recognise soon enough (which means now) what is happening to our homes and family life.

I am, therefore I protest

To all the despair and confusion which has been expressed thus far, a Christian understanding of man has to protest. It is in the very protesting that we assert our true status as children of God. A worker in the North wrote, '*There are millions of people that are concerned about the welfare of our country, and I am one of them. With all respect, Dr. Coggan, a lot of what you say is true but it is not sufficient to say what is wrong, anyone can do that. The main thing to say is how to right the wrong with a definite plan of action.*' He went on to propose a twenty-point programme for national stability.

This was positive. As groups and individuals go on facing all the cataclysmic areas of society-in-charge, and getting involved in the small steps that they can themselves take, they are saying something about man himself. They come back, in effect, to the Archbishop's second question, What sort of people?

If man is made to rise above confusions and failures and defeat, and is here to work out his own answers to the nation's problems, or the world's problems, *he must assert a faith in the possibility of doing so*. He must hang on to it and encourage others to hang on to it. Because that is his nature as a child of God. It is how he and his world were made.

There is a Christian framework to the whole discussion then. Maybe it is in facing ourselves in our society (with all its disappointing side-effects no matter how good our efforts), that our generation

will discover the all-pervasive cancer-like reality of
what the Bible calls 'sin'.

'Sin' in Scripture is essentially a state we belong in
together: a corporate experience and condition. If
our structures reveal their human origin by their
power to confuse and depersonalise, then let us by
all means name names and give new content to old
words and phrases. We are here talking of the social
effects of 'sin', its power to frustrate and destroy us
all. We are talking about a principle behind any of
the small or big 'sins' which may or may not happen
to be important in any one generation or culture.

Against his own cultural background, St. Paul
referred to these forces of dis-array, dis-unity, despair
and confusion, as 'principalities', 'powers', 'domin-
ions', 'spiritual wickedness in high places'. Those
forces over which man felt himself to have no
control, and which indeed seemed poised to take
him over, these Paul *named*.

And in Colossians 2: 15, he says of Jesus Christ
that, 'on the cross he discarded these cosmic powers
and authorities like a garment; he made a public
spectacle of them and led them as captives in his
triumphal procession'. It is an assertion of ultimate,
cosmic, conclusive victory for the forces of resurrection in the face of seeming despair. It is the
statement of why we can go on believing that we can
be co-operators in the creative renewing of our
society.

Sin has only the power to thwart and distract us
until we discover God-in-action within these same
processes that seemed to threaten and inhibit us.

The Archbishop's two questions are one question. And we say as much when we discuss them in groups of differing age, differing background, maybe of differing faith. All of us can be in business about God's Kingdom.

The serious business of adjusting our society to seem fair for all; towards personalness, and the enabling of all our fellow-members to fulfil what is in them to fulfil; anything that says 'no' to 'sin' by refusing to believe we can only give up hope; all this is making statements about that Kingdom.

If you look closely at that list you recognise the outlines of parliamentary programmes and local government agenda. You notice terms reminiscent of the constitutions of many of our voluntary associations. You realise why the Archbishop's 'Call' had to be made to everyone, through the public media, and was not intended as a 'Church' campaign.

The last word should be the Archbishop's. Speaking about the Christian's duties within his nation, when addressing the General Synod of the Church of England soon after the 'Call' was launched, he said:

'Patriotism may well involve the Christian in criticism of his nation and of its governmental policies. But such criticism cannot be given, as it were, from outside. We are part and parcel of our nation, its glory and its shame. Our very loyalty to our nation may have to express itself in terms of criticism, as we bring to bear on it the particular insights God has given to us his children.

'If I give as examples two things of which I have

been speaking much lately, I do so without apology, for I believe they need constant reiteration.

'(a) *The essential sin of our nation is that it has inverted the divine order*. If we do this, putting self first, others next, and God last (if indeed any room is left for him at all), we become idolaters. We assent to the creed of greed. We grasp. We get. We acquire. But we cease to *be* what God designed us to be.

'(b) *If, as a nation, we become obsessed with our rights, then we inevitably come under judgment*. I spoke in Westminster Abbey, of the need of this nation not so much for a charter of *rights* — we have heard much of that — as for a charter of *duties*. When we begin once again to put our accent on that, health will begin to seep back into the veins of our nation. But not till then.

'Perhaps this is England's greatest need today — a band of men and women whose patriotism goes so deep that it leads them to pray, to criticise, to agonise; and out of that prayer, that criticism, that agony, to bear their witness, in season and out of season, to the truth of God as it has been revealed to them in Christ.'